COOKING IN THE

SHAKER SPIRIT

COOKING IN THE SHAKER SPIRIT

JAMES HALLER

WITH JEFFREY PAIGE

YANKEE BOOKS

CAMDEN · MAINE

TEXT AND COVER DESIGN BY LURELLE CHEVERIE

Cover photograph by Ralph Copeland

Typeset by Camden Type 'n Graphics, Camden, Maine

Printed and bound by BookCrafters, Chelsea, Michigan

Library of Congress Cataloging-in-Publication Data

Haller, James.
    Cooking in the Shaker spirit / James Haller, with Jeffrey Paige.
       p.   cm.
    ISBN 0-89909-310-8 : $14.95
    1. Cookery, Shaker.   I. Paige, Jeffrey, 1964–   .   II. Title.
TX715.H182   1990
641.5'088288–dc20   90-42316
                                              CIP

DEDICATION

TO BUD THOMPSON, THE FOREMOST
AUTHORITY ON 20TH-CENTURY SHAKERISM,
WITHOUT WHOSE INTERVENTION CANTERBURY
SHAKER VILLAGE MIGHT HAVE DISAPPEARED;

AND

TO ELDRESS BERTHA LINDSAY, WHO KEEPS THE
FLAME, AND SISTER ETHEL HUDSON, WHO HOLDS
THE LIGHT—A FOND AND LOVING THANK-YOU.

JEFFREY AND I WOULD LIKE TO EXTEND
SPECIAL THANKS TO THE FOLLOWING PEOPLE,
THE CREAMERY STAFF, WHO WAITED
TABLES, WASHED DISHES, MADE DESSERTS,
AND HELPED CUT UP VEGETABLES.

DONNA BEAUPRE	PAT MESSIER
WADE BENNETT	MARY JANE MOULTON
JUDY BORNSTEIN	LOUISE MOORE
CHRISTINA CASSOTIS	RENE PAQUETTE
TERRI FLAHERTY	NAOMI SCANLON
SUKI GOODWIN	BRADY SCHNEIDER
RICHARD KATHMANN	PAM TAYLOR
BRANDON LEBLANC	MICHELLE YORK

CONTENTS

INTRODUCTION
TO THE OLDEST "NEW AMERICAN COOKING"

What makes Shaker cooking the oldest "new American cooking"? There are two reasons. First, the Shakers used locally grown fruits, vegetables, meat, poultry, fish, and dairy products, "taking the ordinary and making it extraordinary." Second, regional Shaker recipes traveled from community to community with improvisations made by the different cooks in each of their kitchens. What began in New England as candied sweet potatoes might have ended up in Kentucky as sweet potato pie. Individual Shakers came from such varied backgrounds that anything regional, ethnic, or even national was adapted to each community and always used the local ingredients. A practice now hailed as "new American cooking" simply was, and is, just using locally grown, fresh ingredients and being as clever with them as the palate and imagination allow.

Probably the qualities that make Shaker cooking uniquely American are its convenience, its simplicity, and its adaptability. That's really what "American style" is to me, certainly in the kitchen.

The Shakers' inventions for the kitchen attest to that. The revolving oven; the corn sheller; the apple peeler, corer, and quarterer; the taffy hook; the egg skimmer; a tin dough box large enough to hold forty loaves of dough to rise; the applesauce tub; the double-roller rolling pins (so that you would have to roll only half as many times); and even the flat broom—all made everyday tasks more efficient and convenient.

If you make whatever needs to be done as convenient as possible, you can invest your energies in making the product wonderful. If you take the drudgery out of the kitchen and fill it with the light of possibility, you can adopt excellence as your tradition and be bound only by the production of quality. That's American style, or it certainly was at one time in our history. The Shakers lived by these tenets for a very long time. They could because their community worked toward the elimination of want and competition among its members.

Instead of competition, the Shakers shared the goal of "Christian perfection," and they sought this perfection in their woodworking, basket making, the making of cloaks and shawls, and the growing of their own herbs for use in their cooking or medicines.

The Shakers knew that if you could make a wonderful product and produce it inexpensively, you could make a fair profit. They baked dozens of pies or pots of beans at one time in their revolving ovens and then delivered them in a horse-drawn cart to stores or families who had ordered them. Often they just parked the cart in the city and sold the goods off the tailgate. There was great demand for Shaker-prepared foods. People could trust the product. They knew it had been made with the best of ingredients and baked with great care. Somehow I never got that sensation while eating Twinkies.

Shaker food was, and still is, by and large, a very healthful cuisine. The evidence of that is the Shakers' records of longevity. Shaker food, however, was not entirely the kind of misinterpretation of health by which we understand food today. Nor was it what one might refer to as a "granola cuisine"; but by the standards of whole, pure, best raised, carefully tended, and heartily enjoyed. Shaker food was indeed healthy. Shakers even kept the floors of their barns as neat as they did their own living quarters because they felt that since an animal was providing them with food, the animal should be cared for with as much concern as a human. This shows a very metaphysical understanding of food, one that I not only ascribe to but teach as well.

The Shakers used great amounts of dairy: buttermilk, milk, and cream in all their heavy, light, soured, whipped, and cottled forms. They used generous amounts of real, homemade butter and copious amounts of sugar. One apple custard pie recipe calls for 1 cup of melted butter, 2 cups of sugar, and 6 eggs. The custard is easily one of my favorites, though I must admit I cut out the butter altogether and used only 1 cup of sugar.

The original recipe is, however, incredibly perfect in taste. It is an utterly rich and energy-filled pastry, and I think it might be okay to have a piece maybe a couple of times a year—but that's because I'm not doing heavy manual labor eight hours a day. I think all food was heavier and richer a hundred years ago because, in the course of an ordinary day, people were able to work it off, if not in actual labor itself, then in the everyday chores of washing, cleaning, cooking, cutting wood, and mowing lawns—all the things that machines now have made easier.

Of course, not all of the cooking contained cream, butter, and sugar. Much of Shaker cooking consisted of salads and clear soups with vegetables, or veal broths with rice. The Shakers also cooked vegetables in ways that one ordinarily would not think of: creamed radishes, or beets in caraway and honey sauce. The Shakers cooked wonderful vegetarian dishes, and they baked a great variety of breads, including bran, wheat, saffron, and fruit breads. These foods were high in energy, low in fat, and always a joy in both taste and concept.

Little sage meat pies, apples filled with custard and wrapped in crust, bacon-and-egg tarts with a creamy top—these were the foods the Shakers packed for picnics or journeys. They created an instant coffee syrup that needed only hot water if the day were cold, or cold water and ice if the day were too warm. At haying time they fixed the brethren a special haying drink called *switchel,* made of barley water, ginger, molasses, and sugar. Sometimes they mixed switchel with ginger ale; often they drank a mixture of iced mint tea and ginger ale. The combination is so refreshing on a hot day that I am convinced that the marriage of ginger and mint was meant as a natural "coolant" to the human system.

For a short time in the 1830s the Shakers, swayed by Sylvester Graham of the cracker notoriety, were convinced that a diet of graham crackers, watered-down milk, and just a few vegetables would soon quell the carnal desires of so many men and women living "together, though apart" in a celibate community. Very soon after the graham diet, other "diets" arrived that not only promised transcending carnal desires but also boasted a direct connection to spirituality in terms of visions and the voices of deceased holy people. Eventually the kitchen Sisters felt that the problems of carnal desires were really the brethren's problems, not theirs, and besides they were tired of making so many different menus. And so, in the early 1840s, the Shakers went back to cooking roasts, birds, and fish. Somewhere along the way they managed to devise forty-nine completely different ways to brilliantly prepare the apple.

It is unfortunate that by the end of the nineteenth century the Shaker movement had begun to recede. The furniture, clothes, tin goods, and basketry became scarce as the community lost the man-and-woman-power to produce these items. By the same token, they began to lose, or find it difficult to recruit people who were talented in the kitchen. It is hard to imagine what Shaker kitchens might be like today if the villages were still flourishing.

Yet the Shaker spirit—those values continue. In these recipes, we use all the foodstuffs the Shakers used but have tried them in new and innovative ways, with one foot in today, in the old-time spirit of Shaker inventiveness and progress. We have put together as varied a menu of recipes as we felt was needed, a mixture of recipes that range from diet-light to healthfully rich; recipes to grace special occasions as well as to use day by day. It may seem a difficult if not contrary notion to understand how a way of cooking that had its basis in being eclectic and adaptive has become a "cuisine." But for some of us, those of us who see cooking not as following a recipe but as understanding a concept, there is certainly a Shaker concept of cooking, just as there is a Shaker concept of making furniture and cabinets, caring for herbs and seeds, and beekeeping.

With the loss of "people power," the Shakers also lost the numbers necessary to till the wonderful gardens, tend the orchards, keep the honeybees, tap the maple trees, tend the cows, keep the dairy running, and raise the chickens, pigs, and sheep—all of the ways the Shakers had been able to remain independent and keep their ethic pure. More and more, the Shakers began to rely on the outside world for survival. This fact, probably more than any other, is what set the Shakers' way of life on its course of demise.

A great part of relying on the outside world had to do with the production, acquisition, and preparation of food. As fewer and fewer recipes came from within the communities, more and more Shaker cooks turned to magazines, newspapers, and cookbooks for new ideas; still they reworked their diminishing stores into inventive concoctions. Where once there were exotic recipes for sherried black bean soup in veal stock with lemon and hard-boiled egg slices, candied lovage root, sausage-stuffed apples, and cold bacon-and-egg pies that came exclusively from Shaker kitchens, there now was food that was easier to prepare either in ingredients or concocting as the few remaining ladies reached their eighties and nineties. Although Shaker cooks no longer had the luxury of homegrown vegetables, homemade butter, and fresh eggs and meats, they still had a flair for ingenuity in their cooking. Eldress Bertha once made lunch for me when she was almost ninety and practically blind. I will never forget it. A blue flower chive omelet in a foldover baking pan, yeast-risen squash biscuits, and a Rosewater Apple Pie. Her cooking was completely on target and was evidence of her talent and years of dedication to and love for the art of cooking.

The reasons the numbers began to dwindle in the Shaker ranks can only be surmised. A great part of it had to do with the fact that after the Civil War more opportunites for people existed. Prior to that if you wanted to stay single, not have a family, there were few alternatives. You could stay on the family farm or get a job working on someone else's farm. If you were a woman, you might enter a convent. Of course, the great alternative for everyone was to go West. You could try your luck in the city but, without a skill or some resource to procure gainful employment, you might end up scrubbing floors or sweeping up horse dung from the streets.

The Shaker community, on the other hand, offered a communal society based on the Shaker principles of "celibacy, community of goods, confession of sin, and withdrawal from the world." In return, the community provided the adherent with a lovely place to live, an abundance of food, manual labor to give a sense of purpose, intellectual development, sanitary living conditions, purity of thought as expressed in speech and personal habits, freedom from all debt and competitiveness, and equality between the sexes. It must be understood, however, that first and foremost it was a religious community. Almost every man, woman, and child in the Shaker community shared the desire to love, serve, and praise God in every act he or she did.

Although there are now only two ladies left at Canterbury Shaker Village in New Hampshire, they remain today as devoted to their faith as they have always been. There are no more services in the meeting house or in the chapel, no prayer gatherings at the holy ground, no form dancing. There is no great community of like-mindedness to lean on or from which to gain support. The kitchen where Eldress Bertha spent most of her life is now inaccessible to her because of failing health. And yet, like her faith, her love for food is as strong as if she were thirty years old. Her delight and surprise in hearing what we concocted on a day's cooking made her laugh and smile as she appreciated, if only for their poetic imagery, our romantic combinations like chilled blueberry lavender buttermilk soup, cumin and maple syrup salad dressing, or broccoli sautéed in gingered apple butter with rose peppercorns.

I am privileged to have known four of the last Shakers at Canterbury. Although tomes have been written about Shaker history, accomplishments, and inventions, my interests have been mainly in my friendships with these women. Two of them still live at Canterbury Shaker Village, the Eldress Bertha Lindsay and Sister Ethel Hudson. They live across the road from one another, Bertha with a live-in companion in the old Trustees' building and Ethel quite alone in rooms occupied until the late 1930s by the last of the Shaker brethren in the enormous building that also houses the chapel. Visits between them are infrequent due to the limitations imposed by their ages, and while they are fondly cordial to one another, it does not seem that they are inclined to close friendship. Ethel says they were not close as children—she was ten when they met, Bertha was eight—and they had little in common other than that they were orphans. Eighty-some years later, the last two Shakers at Canterbury wrap themselves quietly in the comforter of their belief and remain as much Shaker today as they might have been a hundred years ago when their ranks numbered into the thousands.

In the summer of 1988 Eldress Gertrude Soule passed away. The year before that Sister Milly had died.

"She was never a real Shaker," Ethel once told me about Mildred. "No, she never signed the Covenant. Came here when she was sixteen and lived her whole life here till she died at eighty-three, but she never became a Shaker."

Eldress Bertha allows, with a great sense of empathy, that "Mildred was very like a Shaker."

Mildred and her sister were the offspring of an American mother and a Hungarian father. Little is known about them except that one day the father shot the mother to death and went to jail for life. Mildred was sixteen, her sister a year older. They were both sent to the Shaker village at Alfred, Maine, but Mildred was so disruptive the Elders finally asked her to leave. Milly somehow ended up in Canterbury and, when the Elders at Alfred heard she was there, they quickly wrote to suggest that the Canterbury community find another place for her because of her disruptiveness. But the people at Canterbury welcomed Mildred because they knew if they did not, she would find nowhere to stay. Milly continued to be disruptive. Sometimes she acted mean and vex-ing, other times she sewed things for the Sisters, cooked food, made a special basket, then just as quickly became troublesome again. One day in the late 1920s or early 1930s she gathered up her things, packed a bag, and began walking down Shaker Road with the intention of never returning. A younger Sister who had befriended Milly ran after her crying and begging her to stay. Milly returned with the girl and from that day she was Milly's only and close friend.

Over the years I had often seen Milly coming and going quietly, privately, maybe saying a muffled "hello," maybe not. Sometimes she'd be wearing a knit hat pulled down almost to her eyebrows, two sweat-ers, a dress, an extra skirt and jacket, and maybe even a coat over that, with big rubber boots and thick gray knee socks as she darted from building to building, carrying bags, a couple of sacks, and a purse. Sometimes she seemed happy and sweet, sometimes harrassed and busy, but she always had a sense of purpose. Once, after I had given a talk on Shaker Herb Day, she came up to the herbalist and me with a plate of hot dogs and boiled potatoes with butter. "I fixed you a little lunch," she announced. "I liked your talk on herbs. I grow herbs too. You oughta come see my lavender patch sometime." I did, many times.

When Sister Milly died she was buried in the Shaker graveyard in a plot of land that carries a single stone for the scores that rest there. "SHAKERS" it says. Eldress Bertha allows that Milly was "very like a Shaker."

The summers I cooked at Canterbury, I visited Sister Milly's lavender patch almost every day. It covers both sides of the outdoor staircase that leads to what were once her rooms. It is one of the most wonderful lavender patches I have ever seen, and we have used the leaves and blossoms in soups, sauces, salads, and ice creams. Sister Milly was remembered and revered each time the fragrance of lavender filled the kitchen of the Creamery.

The Eldress Gertrude Soule lived to the age of ninty-three. She too arrived as a very young girl and spent most of her life in the Shaker community at Sabbath Day Lake, Maine. For a very short time Gertrude left the community and went out into the world to live. She became a governess in a wealthy home where her innate sense of style and good taste was allowed a freedom not included in the plainness of Shakerism. Although life was pleasant as a governess, Gertrude dearly missed Maine, the Shakers, and the people she had lived with for so many years. She happily returned to Sabbath Day and stayed for almost the rest of her life.

However, life was not meant to remain happy for her. In 1965 the remaining Shakers in the world decided to close the Covenant, thus allowing for the inclusion of no new members. The number of Shakers had dwindled to a handful. The people at Sabbath Day Lake did not agree. They felt it should continue. Eldress Gertrude, however, as a sensible and obedient head of the community, wanted to close the Covenant as had been decided. A disagreement arose, and Gertrude suddenly found herself living with people who were in opposition to her, sometimes unkindly.

In the early 1970s Gertrude visited Canterbury to help one of the older Sisters who was very ill. Within a month or so Gertrude's trunk arrived with a few, scant belongings. None of her photographs, none of her sewing, none of her incredible handiwork. Just some dresses, shoes, and her bonnets. She was asked not to return to Maine. It must have been the most heartbreaking time of her life. But even after that, when she would talk about Sabbath Day Lake, she would always say that she "loved every tree, every blade of grass, every person at Sabbath Day, and held blame to no one." Shakers don't hold blame.

Throughout the years I visited her and had lunch with her, I saw a gentility about Gertrude that has become a rarity—a gentility of decorum and refinement, of polite manners. She was unjudgmental in her perceptions of people, always ready at the defense of the accused, ever seeking a loving explanation or solution to any quandary. She often hugged and kissed me hello and good-bye, always called me "Mr. Haller," and was very pleased that I was cooking at Canterbury.

The last time I saw her I was standing at the kitchen window in the Creamery, washing my hands at the sink. Over the yard and across the road I could see Eldress Gertrude Soule in her Shaker dress and starched cap inspecting the flowers that grow along the fence on the north side of the Trustees' building, picking off blooms that had gone by, and smiling with quiet delight as she smelled the last of the roses. The following afternoon, feeling just a little worn, at the age of ninety-three, Gertrude lay down for a nap and delicately slipped away forever.

And so, in June 1988, there were left the last two Canterbury Shakers, Eldress Bertha Lindsay and Sister Ethel Hudson. They were the end of the line of the Canterbury group that began in 1792.

Sister Ethel's rooms are a strange mixture of furniture, artifacts, paintings, and an untuned upright piano covered with cards and photographs, some new, others soft and yellow-cream colored. There are snapshots of a bright-faced, slender girl with a grin from one corner of her Shaker bonnet to the other that Ethel proudly admits is herself. "That was me when I was but twenty-one, yes." This tiny little cobweb of a woman ninety-three years old—her hair twisted into a thin braid wrapped up the back of her head no longer covered by a starched cap, wearing a faded housedress and little felt slippers—grins the same broad (but now almost toothless) smile, with lights still bright in her blue eyes that, like the dress, have begun to wane in color.

"I came here as a child, my sister and me. Oh, what a long trip it was. Yes, I remember it, all the way by train and then by carriage. I was only eight years old, yes, just a little thing, don't y'know. I was so tired, and when I finally arrived I was set before the Eldress and she looked so sternly down her nose at me, and so I just curtsied, oh very politely like, and looked up at her and said, 'Ma'am, will I do?' " Sister Ethel mimicked the eighty-five-year-old gesture and curtsied politely, eyes fairly dancing with mischief. And then, with a very stern imitation of the old Eldress, Ethel told me, "The Sister looked me over and turned to the other Eldresses and said, 'Well, I can see I have my work cut out for me!' "

Sister Ethel breaks into a laugh at that part of the story, half in amusement, half in defense of her own brashness and spunk. The spunk that arrived with her that tired evening so long ago remained as an intimate and supportive confidante. As a child Ethel felt that the Sisters were stern and concerned with discipline. But discipline was part of what made Shaker order possible. Ethel has always had her own "order."

Today Ethel remains the sole authority of an enormous four-story building of rooms empty save for the dust and litter, as though the millennium the Shakers had been taught to build for had finally arrived. In the hallway, on pegs the Shakers were famous for, hang six or seven of Ethel's dresses, a coat or two, and an old brown pocketbook. It seems that the millennium, like the proverbial last train, has been missed by Sister Ethel Hudson.

When I first met Eldress Bertha Lindsay, she was in her late seventies. Although her eyesight was beginning to fail, her step was agile and her senses easily as alert as anyone's a third her age. She was wearing a blue dress with a print of tiny flowers. It had a bib front, Shaker style, and a little lace trim at the cuffs and collar. On her head, almost like a halo, sat the starched Shaker bonnet. I introduced myself and was completely amazed that Eldress Bertha had heard of me and my cooking. I was particularly interested because she too was a cook. We had an immediate affinity for one another. I asked if I could see her kitchen.

"My kitchen?" The Eldress seemed amused and somewhat puzzled. "Well, yes, if you must."

I was certain I was about to see some wonderful antiquated kitchen filled with ancient utensils and woodstoves or beehive ovens. To my great amazement, the Eldress proudly pointed out a Corning Ware-topped stove that worked with radiant heat, an Osterizer blender, an electric knife sharpener and can opener, and a Mixmaster from the early 1950s. When I told her of my expectations, she laughed. "Why goodness no. The Shakers were very up to date. They had the latest of everything, and what we didn't have we invented to save time and trouble and make the work easier so that we could make the finished product more perfect."

I couldn't have agreed more. I too feel that way about cooking. It should be wonderful and perfect in the outcome, and never a time-consuming, laborious chore.

Through the years the Eldress and I have become friends. My respect for her as a human being (and certainly as a chef) has never waivered. She is a source of inspiration, and has brought to my life a "surviving value." She once told me that she wondered why she was living so long and mused, "What work can I do now?" Those who know her know what work she does. She carries the flame, she keeps it alive, this Shaker fire that began in 1774. Even today she will dress in her Shaker dress and bonnet, and sit in the front hall and greet the people who come to tour the buildings where she once played as a girl. She will tell them about the Shakers in such a way that they know that Canterbury Shaker Village is still very much alive.

I first met Jeffrey Paige in 1981 at a cooking class I was teaching. He was then a seventeen-year-old high-school student who was interested in becoming a chef. The second time I heard from him was seven years later. He called to tell me that he had become a chef and had in fact recently won an award. In a wonderful way he indicated that some of the credit was due to me because he had incorporated much of my approach to food and cooking. He also asked if I wouldn't give a master class to him and his three assistant chefs. Jeffrey's enthusiasm was compelling and so was his food. He offered me a taste of a strawberry-horseradish sauce he had devised for cold shrimp and a chocolate ice cream that contained twenty-five percent butterfat. It was definitely my kind of cooking.

But it is neither the richness of the food nor the novelty of a combination that makes Jeffrey Paige a great cook. It is his sense of taste. It is always the taste that makes a great chef.

Jeffrey eventually applied for the position of assistant chef when he heard I was to be cooking at the Creamery in Canterbury for the summer. Happily for everyone he took the job. Our writing a cookbook together seemed the most natural outcome of a very happy time. And so, in the following pages, we offer a variety of dishes that we cooked in the Shaker spirit of inventiveness, care, and simplicity. To anyone who loves cooking, here is a taste of a very happy time.

HERBS

The Shakers used almost exclusively only four herbs in the kitchen. Parsley, mint, sage, and thyme—an amazing fact considering they cultivated hundreds of others for medicinal purposes. This Spartan array in the kitchen may be a holdover from the early Puritans who felt that herbs and spices were gifts from the devil used in making witchcraft potions or aphrodisiacs. (This also explains why New England cooking is generally on the bland side.) Another explanation may be that some herbs, like basil, were not generally introduced into this country until the middle of the nineteenth century.

We used as many herbs as we could grow when putting together this cookbook. For those of you who are not familiar with a certain herb or spice and want to try it, the best way is to mix it into mashed potatoes. The potato seems to be the most accommodating vegetable for conveying the taste of herbs. Another idea is to sauté tofu in olive oil with fresh herbs. Tofu, the chameleon of the kitchen, will assume the taste of whatever it is cooked with.

Stimulating taste and excitement and making mundane foods into new treats are just a few reasons to explore the world of herbs, whether they are fresh or dried. They can also help in digestion, carry trace vitamins, and substitute for condiments that might not agree with you. You can grow herbs in a window box, in a flower pot, or on any half-decent available plot of land. Remember that herbs are basically a weed and don't need extraordinary care.

SUBSTITUTIONS

In some recipes you might want to substitute milk or even skim milk for cream or light cream, yogurt for sour cream, or kefir for buttermilk. The recipe will taste slightly altered but will, nonetheless, still be a great recipe. But this is not a "diet" cookbook. I personally feel that all food, as long as it is whole, pure, fresh, and unrefined, is healthful. The secret to any diet is simply to eat less. Furthermore, what might work for one person very possibly might not work for someone else. Metabolism, physical makeup, emotional needs, and activities all play a part.

North Americans have been hyped by Madison Avenue into a state of fear of eating. The "health experts" seem to be advertising copywriters, the nutritionists (who generally know nothing about cooking), and the media who prefer to sell half-truths about everything in order to sell.

For instance, there is this great debate over the deadly cholesterol content of butter. We are admonished, instead, to eat margarine. Yes, margarine has less cholesterol, and nothing else. No food value and the same number of calories. Butter, on the other hand, is loaded with protein, vitamin A, and other life-giving and life-supporting nutrients. Does this mean I'm telling you to eat a quarter-pound of butter a day? Of course not. What I'm saying is that butter is far tastier than margarine and far more healthful. If you have a little in the morning on toast or pancakes, you have the rest of the day to work it off. In the meantime you've eaten something that is really beneficial to you. Of course, if you do have a cholesterol problem, don't eat butter. Most important, learn to think for yourself. Like the Shakers, remove yourself from the world—in this case, the world of misinformation, fear, and stress that advertising hype can produce. And when you do, fix yourself a lovely pot of soup from this truly unique collection of Creamery recipes.

S O U P S

In the first section the soups listed may be served either hot or cold. Any leftover soups can be turned into innovative salad dressings simply by adding a little vinegar and oil and stirring well.

SISTER MILLY'S LAVENDER

RADISH CREAM SOUP

SERVES 6–8

This soup has its beginnings as an old Shaker recipe for a spinach ring filled with creamed radishes. The radish is generally found in salads, but when I read of its use in the spinach ring, I was inspired to take a further step. The addition of the lavender is in memory of Sister Milly.

2 CUPS RED RADISHES	1 PINT HEAVY CREAM
1 STICK UNSALTED BUTTER	1 PINT LIGHT CREAM
½ CUP FLOUR	2–3 LAVENDER SPRIGS
1 CUP WHITE WINE	

Wash, trim, and slice the radishes (measure 2 cups after slicing). Melt the butter in a soup pot. Slowly cook the radishes 5–7 minutes. Add the flour, stirring well to form a roux. Stir in the white wine and heavy and light creams, blending until smooth. Add the lavender sprigs and simmer the soup for 30 minutes. Season with salt and pepper. Serve.

CORN CHOWDER

I don't think any New England–based cookbook would be complete without a recipe for corn chowder. This one is simple, fast, and better than anyone else's—except of course for the one you're about to make. Part of what makes it so delicious is the use of bacon grease. What may sound like a ton of fat and cholesterol is really only a smattering of drippings that will be divided up among six to eight people. So relax and enjoy the taste of what cooking used to be.

1 MEDIUM ONION, DICED	2 CUPS CORN KERNELS
IN HALF-INCH PIECES	WHITE WINE TO COVER
1/2 POUND BACON, DICED	1 QUART MILK
2 MEDIUM POTATOES, DICED	
IN HALF-INCH PIECES	

In a soup pot fry the onions and bacon until crisp. Drain off half of the bacon fat. Add the potatoes, corn, and white wine to cover. Simmer the chowder until the potatoes are soft. Add the milk, and season with salt and pepper. Puree 1 cup of the chowder in a blender and return the puree to the soup pot. Serve.

TOMATO APPLE SOUP

SERVES 6–8

At the height of the Canterbury community, the Shakers grew over a hundred different varieties of apples. In one of their cookbooks I found forty-nine different recipes for apples. The apple was, in fact, one of the chief supports of the community. Even today in the orchard just past the meeting house and the ministry building, trees still grow and bear fruit after more than a hundred years. We offer yet a few more ways to use this sacred fruit.

1 MEDIUM ONION, CHOPPED	1 QUART BEEF STOCK
12 MEDIUM TOMATOES,	3 APPLES, PEELED AND SHREDDED
QUARTERED	1 TABLESPOON CINNAMON
1 CUP WHITE WINE	

In a stockpot simmer the chopped onion and tomatoes in the wine and stock for 45–60 minutes. Strain the soup, and return the liquid to a soup pot. Add the shredded apples and cinnamon, and season with salt and pepper. Simmer the soup for 10–15 minutes and serve.

TOMATO APPLE

HERB SOUP

SERVES 6–8

1/2 STICK UNSALTED BUTTER	2 APPLES, PEELED AND SHREDDED
1/2 CUP MINCED ONION	1 CUP CHOPPED TOMATOES
1/2 CUP FLOUR	2 TABLESPOONS DILL
2 CUPS CHICKEN STOCK	2 CUPS LIGHT CREAM
2 CUPS TOMATO SAUCE	

In a soup pot melt the butter and sauté the minced onion. Add the flour, and stir to form a roux. Stir in the stock and tomato sauce, blending until smooth. Add the apples, chopped tomatoes, and dill. Simmer the soup for 30–45 minutes. Season with salt and pepper. Finish the soup by blending in the light cream at serving time.

SHERRIED BLACK BEAN SOUP

WITH LEMON AND EGG GARNISH

———

SERVES 6–8

This recipe begins in Mary Witcher's *Shaker Housekeeping Book*. I thought it was very sophisticated for the time because the recipe instructs you to line the tureen with thin slices of lemon and hard-boiled egg and then pour in the soup. The instructions were wonderfully simple. "Boil one quart of black beans with three quarts of water and a veal knuckle." The trick here is to find a "veal knuckle." I spoke with five butchers, and none of them knew what a veal knuckle was. I would have thought the knee joint. I settled for a veal breast. The sherry can be added anytime—the closer to serving time, the more sherry taste, which, in this soup, is wonderful. I found the soup particularly interesting because it was a bean soup that didn't begin with a ham bone or pork base.

1 QUART DRIED BLACK BEANS	1 MEDIUM ONION, CHOPPED
2½ QUARTS WATER	2 MEDIUM TOMATOES, CHOPPED
2 POUNDS VEAL BREAST OR	1 LEMON, THINLY SLICED
1 POUND BACON	2 HARD-BOILED EGGS, CHOPPED
2 CUPS SHERRY WINE	

Soak the beans in the water overnight in the refrigerator. Pour the beans, water, veal, sherry, onion, and tomatoes into a soup pot. Simmer the soup, cooking until the beans are tender for 1½–2 hours. Add more water if necessary. Remove the veal breast if you used veal. Puree 2–3 cups of the soup, and return the puree to the soup pot. Season with salt and pepper. To serve, place a lemon slice in each bowl, ladle in the soup, and garnish with chopped hard-boiled eggs.

CREAM OF ASPARAGUS SOUP

SERVES 6–8

2 POUNDS ASPARAGUS, TIPS REMOVED

1 TABLESPOON MINCED GARLIC

1 MEDIUM ONION, CHOPPED

1 CUP WHITE WINE

1 CUBE CHICKEN BOUILLON

1 CUP MILK

2 CUPS HEAVY CREAM

Remove tips from asparagus and set tips aside for steaming later. In a soup pot simmer the asparagus spears, garlic, and onion in the wine, bouillon, and milk until soft for 20–30 minutes. Puree the soup in a blender until smooth. Return the soup to the soup pot, add the cream, and season with salt and pepper. Steam asparagus tips. Serve the soup garnished with the asparagus tips.

SUMMER VEGETABLE

CREAM SOUP

SERVES 6–8

1 STICK UNSALTED BUTTER	1/2 CUP FLOUR
1 TABLESPOON MINCED GARLIC	3 CUPS CHICKEN STOCK
2 CUPS SUMMER VEGETABLES,	1 CUP LIGHT CREAM
CHOPPED (NO TOMATOES)	1 CUP HEAVY CREAM

Melt the butter in a soup pot, and cook the garlic and chopped vegetables 7–10 minutes. Add the flour, and stir to make a roux. Add the stock, stirring until smooth. Simmer the soup 30 minutes. Add the creams, season with salt and pepper, and serve.

SHAKER HERB BROTH

SERVES 6–8

2 QUARTS BEEF STOCK

1 CUP RED WINE

4 MEDIUM TOMATOES,
CHOPPED

1 TABLESPOON MINCED
ROSEMARY

1 TABLESPOON MINCED THYME

1 TABLESPOON MINCED SAGE

1 TABLESPOON CUMIN

3 BAY LEAVES

Combine all of the ingredients in a soup pot. Bring the soup to a simmer, and cook 1 hour. Remove bay leaves. Puree in a blender until smooth. Season with salt and pepper. Serve.

ZUCCHINI AND LEEK SOUP

SERVES 6–8

After "What came first, the chicken or the egg?" I think the second most unanswerable question is, "God, what'll we do with all this zucchini?" Everyone has some brilliant suggestion; in fact, there is even a cookbook out on zucchini cooking.

Zucchini isn't a powerhouse of nutrients, though it does have a fair amount of potassium and vitamin A. And though I've eaten it shredded, raw, cooked, breaded and sautéed with olive oil and garlic, mixed into wonderful ratatouilles, stuffed in a hundred different ways, and even in a couple of chocolate cakes, I'm still not completely impressed with zucchini. I don't grow it. There's plenty around. Somebody always grows too much and inevitably asks that second unanswerable question. Sooner or later I come up with an answer.

1 STICK UNSALTED BUTTER	2 CUPS CHICKEN STOCK
2 CUPS MINCED LEEKS	2 CUPS SHREDDED ZUCCHINI
1/2 CUP FLOUR	4 CUPS LIGHT CREAM
1 CUP WHITE WINE	2 TEASPOONS NUTMEG

Melt the butter in a soup pot, and cook the leeks until soft. Add the flour, and stir to make a roux. Add the wine and stock, stirring until smooth. Add the shredded zucchini, and simmer for 30 minutes. Add the cream and nutmeg, season with salt and pepper, and serve.

DARK TOMATO BASIL

ONION SOUP

SERVES 6–8

1 QUART BEEF STOCK	4 MEDIUM TOMATOES, PEELED,
2 MEDIUM ONIONS, THINLY	SEEDED, AND CHOPPED
SLICED	1 CUP MINCED FRESH BASIL
2 TABLESPOONS MINCED GARLIC	$1/2$ CUP SHREDDED CARROT

Combine all of the ingredients in a soup pot. Simmer the soup for 30–45 minutes. Season with salt and pepper, and serve.

SHERRIED PUMPKIN

APPLE SOUP

SERVES 6–8

This soup is another that is as wonderful hot as it is cold. If you are serving it cold, a dollop of sour cream or yogurt added to each serving is a great finishing touch.

½ STICK UNSALTED BUTTER	2 CUPS PUMPKIN PUREE
1 TABLESPOON MINCED GARLIC	3 CUPS LIGHT CREAM
1 CUBE CHICKEN BOUILLON	2 APPLES, PEELED AND SHREDDED
1 CUP SHERRY	1 TABLESPOON NUTMEG

Melt the butter in a soup pot, and cook the garlic for 1 minute. Add the remaining ingredients except the apples and nutmeg. Simmer for 30 minutes. Add the apples and nutmeg just before serving time. Season with salt and pepper, and serve.

SHAKER-STYLE

FISH CHOWDER

———

SERVES 6–8

¹/₂ POUND BACON, DICED	WATER TO COVER
1 CUP DICED ONION	3 CUPS CUBED WHITEFISH
2 MEDIUM POTATOES, PEELED	3 CUPS LIGHT CREAM
AND DICED	¹/₂ CUP CRACKER* CRUMBS

Fry the bacon in a soup pot. Drain off half of the grease. Add the onions, potatoes, and water to cover. Simmer the soup until the potatoes are soft. Add the fish and cream. Simmer 5–7 minutes until the fish is cooked. Season with salt and pepper. At serving time add the cracker crumbs.

*Use your favorite cracker to make the cracker crumbs or experiment with Vermont common crackers, oyster crackers, or Ritz crackers to find out which you like best.

SHAKER THREE BEAN

CHOWDER

SERVES 6–8

½ CUP DRIED YELLOW SPLIT PEAS	1 CUP DICED ONION
½ CUP DRIED BLACK BEANS	4 CUPS TOMATOES IN JUICE (CANNED)
½ CUP DRIED LENTILS	2 TABLESPOONS MINCED GARLIC
4 CUPS WATER	1 CUP RED WINE
1 CUP DICED HAM	1 CUP SHERRY
1 MEDIUM POTATO, PEELED AND DICED	

Soak the beans and lentils in the water overnight in the refrigerator. Combine the remaining ingredients in a soup pot. Simmer the soup until the beans and potatoes are soft, about 2 hours. Add more water if necessary. Season with salt and pepper. Serve.

SHIITAKE MUSHROOM

ONION SOUP

SERVES 6–8

There seems to be no mention of shiitake mushrooms in old Shaker recipes, though many Shaker recipes call for mushrooms. The Shakers certainly knew about the wild foods available because of their tenet toward inventiveness. Even now in the fields that surround Canterbury Shaker Village there are wild mushrooms, fiddlehead ferns, wild herbs, and other weeds and flowers that Shakers used in their daily life—both for their own use and in the products they sold to the public. We think this is a soup they might have made if they were using wild mushrooms. Fortunately today "shiitake" mushrooms are available in almost any supermarket.

1 STICK UNSALTED BUTTER	1/2 CUP FLOUR
2 CUPS ONION, THINLY SLICED	3 CUPS BEEF BOUILLON
3 CUPS SLICED SHIITAKE	1 CUP LIGHT CREAM
MUSHROOMS	1 CUP HEAVY CREAM

In a soup pot melt the butter and cook the onions 1–2 minutes. Add the sliced mushrooms, and cook 1–2 minutes. Stir in the flour to make a roux. Add the bouillon, stirring until smooth. Simmer the soup for 30 minutes. Add the creams, season with salt and pepper, and serve.

CHILLED SOUPS

CHILLED SORREL CREAM SOUP

WITH FLAKED SALMON

SERVES 6–8

The summer of 1988 in New England was the hottest I have ever known. The temperatures at the Shaker Village from August until mid-September often ranged into the top 90s and past the 100-degree mark. Of course, in a kitchen with four ovens going at one time, to say nothing of the exhaust from refrigerators and coolers working overtime, the temperature often felt like 115 degrees. I had two firsts in the kitchen that summer. One was to cook my first meal without a trace of wine or liquor throughout the entire dinner, and the second, thanks to a soaring thermometer, was to prepare entire cold dinners. The latter idea became very intriguing to me and afforded a completely new field of experimentation. This soup was part of that experiment.

1 CUP MINCED LEEKS	2 CUPS CHOPPED SORREL
1 STICK UNSALTED BUTTER OR	1 CUP LIGHT CREAM
1/2 CUP BACON GREASE	1 CUP BUTTERMILK
1/2 CUP FLOUR	2 CUPS SALMON, COOKED,
1 CUP SHERRY OR WHITE WINE	CHILLED, AND FLAKED
2 CUPS MILK	

Wash and slice the leeks. In a soup pot cook the leeks in the butter or bacon grease for 2–3 minutes. Add the flour and stir to make a roux. Add the sherry or white wine, milk, and chopped sorrel, stirring until smooth. Simmer the soup for 30 minutes. Chill 24 hours. Add the cream, buttermilk, and flaked salmon. Season with salt and pepper. Serve in chilled bowls.

CHILLED BLUEBERRY LAVENDER

BUTTERMILK SOUP

SERVES 6–8

This recipe really began as a sauce for chocolate pudding. The color, sort of an electric lavender, was as vivid as the taste. Not only did we think it would be unique as a sauce over pudding, but we also thought that surely no one else in the state of New Hampshire would be concocting such a thing on such an evening. In the middle of our self-congratulations the Village director wandered into the kitchen wearing, amazingly enough, a shirt that exactly matched the color of the sauce. Jeff and I smugly and proudly offered him a spoonful to taste. His face lit up and he said, "It's delicious! What a great idea for such a hot evening. A chilled blueberry soup!" It took Jeff and me only a moment to realize that another great idea had been born. We added a couple of cups of buttermilk, and that evening, instead of ending the dinner as a dessert this new creation began it.

4 PINTS BLUEBERRIES	6–8 LAVENDER SPRIGS
2 CUPS MAPLE SYRUP	2 CUPS BUTTERMILK
JUICE OF 1 LEMON	2 CUPS LIGHT CREAM

Pick through and wash the blueberries. In a soup pot combine the berries, maple syrup, and lemon juice. Simmer the mixture for 30 minutes. Puree the soup in a blender until smooth. Chill. Soak the lavender sprigs in the buttermilk and cream for 45–60 minutes, then strain. Combine the chilled soup base with the perfumed cream and buttermilk mixture. Chill the soup 4 hours before serving to allow flavors to develop. Serve in chilled bowls garnished with blueberry lavender ice cubes. For the ice cubes, fill a conventional ice cube tray with lavender blossoms and blueberry juice, then freeze.

CHILLED MINTED CUCUMBER

BUTTERMILK SOUP

SERVES 6–8

The Canterbury Shakers had one of the finest herds of Guernseys in the country, and legend has it that their cream was so thick that you could stand a fork up in it immediately after separating it from the milk. There is evidence in Shaker cookbooks of the generous use of milk products, including buttermilk; one of the most popular herbs was mint. Combining the two seemed a natural for this recipe.

Somewhere along the way people stopped drinking buttermilk. You almost can't find it in stores anymore. It's tart, refreshing, and healthy. One cup has about a hundred calories, provides about eight grams of protein, and is high in phosphorus, potassium, and calcium.

2 MEDIUM CUCUMBERS	2 CUPS CHICKEN STOCK
1 STICK UNSALTED BUTTER	2 TABLESPOONS CHOPPED MINT
2 TABLESPOONS MINCED	1 CUP LIGHT CREAM
GARLIC	2 CUPS BUTTERMILK
1/2 CUP FLOUR	PLAIN YOGURT
1 CUP WHITE WINE	

Peel, seed, and dice the cucumbers. Melt the butter in a soup pot, and cook the cucumbers and garlic 3–5 minutes. Add the flour, stirring to make a roux. Add the wine and stock, stirring until smooth. Add the chopped mint. Simmer the soup for 15 minutes. Chill this mixture . Finish the cold soup base by blending in the cream and buttermilk. Season with salt and pepper. Serve each bowl of soup with a dollop of yogurt.

CHILLED SORREL AND CUCUMBER

BUTTERMILK SOUP

SERVES 6–8

2 MEDIUM CUCUMBERS	1 CUP WHITE WINE
1 STICK UNSALTED BUTTER	2 CUPS CHOPPED SORREL
1/2 CUP FLOUR	2 CUPS BUTTERMILK
2 1/2 CUPS CHICKEN STOCK	

Peel, seed, and dice the cucumbers. Melt the butter in a soup pot, and cook the cucumbers for 3–5 minutes. Add the flour, and stir to make a roux. Add the stock and wine, stirring until smooth. Add the chopped sorrel, and simmer the soup for 20–30 minutes. Chill this mixture. Finish the soup by stirring in the buttermilk, and season with salt and pepper. Serve in chilled bowls. Variation: Add 1–2 tablespoons minced ginger root.

CHILLED SHERRIED

SALMON CHOWDER

SERVES 6–8

2 MEDIUM POTATOES	WATER TO COVER
½ CUP CHOPPED ONION	3 CUPS CUBED SALMON FILLET
1 STICK UNSALTED BUTTER	2 TABLESPOONS MINCED
2 TABLESPOONS LOBSTER	TARRAGON
BOUILLON	3 CUPS LIGHT CREAM
2 CUPS SHERRY	1 CUP BUTTERMILK

Peel and dice the potatoes. In a soup pot cook the onions in the butter 2–3 minutes. Add the potatoes, lobster bouillon, sherry, and enough water to cover the potatoes. Simmer the soup until the potatoes start to soften. Add the cubed salmon and minced tarragon. Cook until the salmon starts to fall apart. Remove the soup from the stove and chill 24 hours. Finish the soup by blending in the cream and buttermilk, and season with salt and pepper. Serve in chilled bowls.

SALADS AND SALAD DRESSINGS

How wonderful it is to grow and eat your own fresh food right out of the earth. I have always felt that fresh vegetables and fruits and herbs are our connection to perfect order. I say this because it seems the universe runs in perfect order. Every year there is a spring, summer, fall, and winter. It never changes. From this perfect order comes new growth and from growth progress. You can pick an apple, or dig a potato or beet, or pluck a Brussels sprout and eat it. It is your connection to perfect order. And every time you use an imitation or a substitute or eat some processed piece of fast food you put a wall between you and that perfect order. In this whole milieu of fruits and vegetables and herbs and spices and natural oils and saps lies the cure for all of the physical ailments in the world. I believe it must be so. Food is our fuel. It's what we must have to make us work. I think the Shakers had an understanding of this. I see evidence of it in their cooking and herb production.

In their tradition, Jeffrey and I devised salads and dressings that use locally grown foods and incorporate some of the more exotic herbs and spices the Shakers might have imported.

At the Canterbury community maple sugar and syrup were generously used, along with their own selection of flavored honeys. Unfortunately this is a practice that has become a victim of time. These products no longer come from the village, but are made at neighboring farms from trees and fields that once belonged to the Shakers.

HERBED MAPLE SYRUP

DRESSING

———

²/₃ CUP OLIVE OIL

¹/₃ CUP WHITE WINE VINEGAR

¹/₃ CUP MAPLE SYRUP

1 TABLESPOON MINCED CHIVES

1 TABLESPOON MINCED PARSLEY

1 TABLESPOON MINCED

TARRAGON

Combine all of the ingredients in a blender, and mix for 30 seconds. Refrigerate 3 hours before using.

CUMIN MAPLE SYRUP

DRESSING

---

²/₃ CUP OLIVE OIL

¹/₃ CUP WHITE WINE VINEGAR

¹/₃ CUP MAPLE SYRUP

1 TABLESPOON DIJON MUSTARD

1–2 TEASPOONS CUMIN

Combine all of the ingredients in a blender, and mix for 30 seconds. Refrigerate 3 hours before using.

ONION MAPLE SUGAR

VINAIGRETTE

---

1 1/2 CUPS OLIVE OIL

1/2 CUP WHITE WINE VINEGAR

1/2 CUP MAPLE SUGAR OR

   MAPLE SYRUP

1/2 CUP CHOPPED ONION

1 1/2 TEASPOONS MINCED BASIL

1 1/2 TEASPOONS MINCED OREGANO

1 TEASPOON MARJORAM

Combine all of the ingredients in a blender, and puree until a fine-textured dressing remains. Season with salt and pepper. Refrigerate 3 hours before using.

SLICED ZUCCHINI

IN A MAPLE VINAIGRETTE

———

2 MEDIUM ZUCCHINI, SLICED

1 MEDIUM ONION, THINLY
    SLICED

1/2 CUP WHITE WINE VINEGAR

1 CUP MAPLE SYRUP

1/4 CUP DIJON MUSTARD

JUICE OF 1 LEMON

1 TABLESPOON MINCED GARLIC

1 TABLESPOON CURRY POWDER

Toss the sliced zucchini and onion together in a bowl. Combine
the remaining ingredients in a blender, and mix for 30 seconds.
Mix the vegetables with the dressing, and serve.

APPLE

Since the Shakers devised so many recipes for the apple, it was interesting (and fun) for us to come up with new (and credible) ideas. We feel we succeeded.

APPLE SOUR CREAM

DRESSING

1/2 POUND BACON	1/4 CUP CIDER VINEGAR
3/4 CUP FROZEN APPLE JUICE CONCENTRATE	2 TABLESPOONS MINCED GARLIC
2 CUPS SOUR CREAM OR YOGURT	2 TABLESPOONS MINCED CHIVES

Slice the bacon into bites, and fry until crisp. Drain. Combine the bacon and remaining ingredients in a food processor. Blend using the pulse button 30–45 seconds. Refrigerate 3 hours before using. Serve over chilled blanched asparagus.

APPLE AND CUCUMBER SALAD

WITH A SWEET AND

SOUR GINGER DRESSING

---

2 MEDIUM CUCUMBERS	JUICE OF 1 LEMON
2 CORTLAND APPLES	1/2 CUP HONEY
1 CUP SALAD OIL	2 TABLESPOONS GRATED
1/3 CUP WHITE WINE VINEGAR	GINGER ROOT

Wash, peel, seed, and slice the cucumbers. Wash, core, and slice the apples. Combine the remaining ingredients in a blender, and mix for 30 seconds. In a bowl toss the sliced cucumbers and apples with the dressing. Season with salt and pepper. Serve.

SHREDDED APPLES

IN A CRANBERRY ORANGE

PECAN DRESSING

1 FOURTEEN-OUNCE CAN OF

    WHOLE CRANBERRIES

    IN JELLY

1/4 CUP FROZEN ORANGE JUICE

    CONCENTRATE

JUICE OF 1 LEMON

1 CUP PECAN PIECES

6 MCINTOSH APPLES

LETTUCE CUPS

Combine the cranberries, orange juice concentrate, lemon juice, and pecan pieces in a food processor, and process using the pulse button for 15–30 seconds. Wash, core, and shred the apples in a food processor. Combine the dressing and apples, tossing well. Serve the salad in individual lettuce cups.

TART APPLE AND PEPPER

SALAD WITH A

WARM BACON DRESSING

½ POUND BACON	1 TABLESPOON CURRY POWDER
1 MEDIUM ONION, DICED	OR CHOPPED SPEARMINT
1 CUP MAPLE SYRUP	4 CORTLAND APPLES
½ CUP CIDER VINEGAR	2 BELL PEPPERS, (RED, GREEN,
	YELLOW, OR ORANGE)

Slice the bacon into bites. In a sauce pot fry the bacon, adding the diced onion halfway through the cooking. Drain off half of the bacon grease. Add the maple syrup, vinegar, and curry powder or chopped spearmint. Simmer the dressing for 15 minutes. Wash, core, and slice the apples. Wash, seed, and thinly slice the peppers. Combine the sliced apples and bell peppers in a bowl, and toss with the dressing. Season with salt and pepper, and serve immediately.

BAKED CORTLAND APPLE CHILLED IN A SWEET AND SOUR DRESSING

---

4 CORTLAND APPLES	1 TABLESPOON MINCED
3/4 CUP MAPLE SYRUP	SPEARMINT
1/4 CUP CIDER VINEGAR	LETTUCE LEAVES

Wash, core, and halve the apples. Place in a baking dish. Combine the syrup, vinegar, and spearmint in a blender, and mix for 30 seconds. Pour the dressing over the apples. Bake in a 400° F oven for 10 minutes or until the apples start to soften (be careful not to overcook them). Place the baking dish in the refrigerator to chill. To serve, place a washed lettuce leaf on each plate, thinly slice half an apple per person, fan the apple slices across the lettuce, and drizzle with the sweet and sour dressing.

SPINACH SALAD WITH

A WARM SWEET AND

SOUR APPLE DRESSING

————

2 POUNDS FRESH SPINACH	1/2–3/4 CUP HONEY
2 CORTLAND APPLES	1 MEDIUM ONION, MINCED
1 CUP OLIVE OIL	1 TABLESPOON MINCED GARLIC
1/4 CUP APPLE CIDER	1 TABLESPOON MINCED ROSEMARY
1/4 CUP CIDER VINEGAR	1 TABLESPOON MINCED SAGE
JUICE OF 1 LEMON	1 BAY LEAF

Remove stems from, wash, and dry the spinach. Set aside. Wash and core the apples, then shred in a food processor. Combine apples and remaining ingredients in a sauce pot. Simmer the dressing until reduced by one-third. Ladle the warm dressing over the spinach, and serve immediately.

SAUTÉED VEGETABLE SALAD CHILLED IN A SWEET AND SOUR CUMIN DRESSING

---

1 CUP DICED ZUCCHINI

1 CUP DICED SUMMER SQUASH

1 CUP DICED GREEN PEPPER

1 CUP CHOPPED TOMATOES,

    SEEDED

$^1/_4$ CUP OLIVE OIL

$^1/_2$ CUP BROWN SUGAR

1 TABLESPOON CUMIN

$^1/_2$ CUP WHITE WINE VINEGAR

Wash all of the vegetables. Diced pieces should be no larger than half an inch. Heat the oil in a large frying pan or a wok. Quickly cook the vegetables for 3–5 minutes. Dissolve the brown sugar and cumin in the vinegar. Add to the pan with the vegetables, and stir in well. Remove pan from the stove, transfer vegetables to a bowl, and refrigerate. Season with salt and pepper, and serve.

CRANBERRY PEAR

SORBET ON SHREDDED

FRESH SPINACH

———

6 MEDIUM PEARS	GRANULATED SUGAR TO TASTE
1 CUP CRANBERRIES	1 POUND FRESH SPINACH

Wash, core, and quarter the pears. Pick over and wash the cranberries. Place the pears and cranberries in a food processor and puree, adding the sugar to taste. Pour the mixture into a container, and freeze overnight. To serve, remove the sorbet from the freezer 10–15 minutes prior to serving, and place a scoop on individual beds of picked over, washed, and shredded fresh spinach.

PEAR

MAYONNAISE

---

2 MEDIUM PEARS	1 TABLESPOON LIME JUICE
1 CUP MAYONNAISE	1 TABLESPOON MINCED GARLIC
2 TABLESPOONS HONEY	

Wash, core, and quarter the pears. Combine pears and remaining
ingredients in a food processor, and puree until smooth.
Refrigerate 3 hours before using. Serve over fresh garden greens
or vegetable salad.

SLICED TOMATOES

WITH A MINTED

ORANGE DRESSING

---

4 MEDIUM TOMATOES	1/2 CUP HONEY
1 CUP FROZEN ORANGE JUICE	JUICE OF 1/2 LEMON
CONCENTRATE	1/2 CUP FRESH SPEARMINT
1/2 ORANGE, SLICED AND	
SEEDED	

Wash, core, and slice the tomatoes (use half a tomato per person). Combine the remaining ingredients in a blender, and mix for 30 seconds. Ladle the dressing over the sliced tomatoes, and serve.

OPTIONAL: 1 CUP MAYONNAISE | 1 PINT FRESH RASPBERRIES

Add mayonnaise and raspberries when blending the dressing.

LEMON SAFFRON

VINAIGRETTE

———

3 CUPS OLIVE OIL

1 CUP WHITE WINE VINEGAR

1 CUP FRESH LEMON JUICE

$1/4$ CUP HONEY

2 TABLESPOONS MINCED

GARLIC

1 TABLESPOON WATER

1 TEASPOON SAFFRON

Combine all of the ingredients in a blender, and mix for
30 seconds. Refrigerate for 3 hours before using.

SLICED CUCUMBERS

WITH MINTED

LEMONADE DRESSING

---

2 LEMONS, SLICED AND SEEDED

1 CUP WHITE WINE

3 CUPS GRANULATED SUGAR

$\frac{1}{4}$ CUP SPEARMINT

3 MEDIUM CUCUMBERS

In a sauce pot combine the lemons, wine, and sugar. Simmer until reduced by half. Place the mixture in a food processor. Add the spearmint, and puree 15–30 seconds. Chill. Wash, peel, seed, and slice the cucumbers. Toss with the minted lemonade puree, and serve.

SLICED CUCUMBERS

WITH A LEMON

SOUR CREAM DRESSING

---

4 LEMONS, SLICED AND SEEDED

1 CUP GRANULATED SUGAR

$1/2$ CUP FRESH SPEARMINT

1 PINT SOUR CREAM

$1/2$–$3/4$ CUP WHITE WINE VINEGAR

3 MEDIUM CUCUMBERS

Combine the lemon slices, sugar, and spearmint in a food processor, and chop roughly. Stir in the sour cream. Stir in the vinegar to taste. Refrigerate 3 hours before using. Wash, peel, seed, and slice the cucumbers. Toss the cucumbers with the dressing, and serve. Also goes nicely with a seasonal garden salad.

CUCUMBER AND BACON SALAD WITH SUMMER SPEARMINT VINAIGRETTE

———

As soon as you say "spearmint" people invariably think of chewing gum. But the herb used in different ways becomes very unlike the taste of chewing gum when you allow yourself the freedom to experiment. The uses for the following recipe vary from a salad dressing to a fruit dressing, or a sauce for a cold shrimp or fish salad. You can even marinate scallops in this sauce overnight and serve them raw and chilled as a seviche.

1/2 POUND BACON	3 TABLESPOONS FRESH
2/3 CUP OLIVE OIL	SPEARMINT
1/3 CUP WHITE WINE VINEGAR	3 MEDIUM CUCUMBERS
1/3 CUP HONEY	

Dice the bacon, and fry until crisp. Drain. Combine the oil, vinegar, honey, and spearmint in a blender, and mix for 30 seconds. Wash, peel, seed, and slice the cucumbers. Toss the cucumbers, crisp bacon, and vinaigrette. Season with salt and pepper, and serve.

These last six salads are the ones that elicited the most praise from the other people who worked in the Creamery kitchen and dining room. In all actuality, it was these "other people" who always had the final okay on any recipe. These were the people who waited on tables, washed dishes, made desserts, and helped cut up vegetables.

CORN AND BLUEBERRY

SALAD IN A CURRIED

ORANGE DRESSING

———

1 CUP FROZEN ORANGE JUICE
CONCENTRATE

1/8 CUP WHITE WINE VINEGAR

1/4 CUP MAPLE SYRUP

JUICE OF 1/2 LIME

1 TABLESPOON CURRY POWDER

4 CUPS CORN

2 CUPS BLUEBERRIES

Combine the orange juice concentrate, vinegar, maple syrup, lime juice, and curry powder in a blender, and mix for 30 seconds. Toss the corn, blueberries, and dressing. Season with salt and pepper, and serve.

STRAWBERRY AND CUCUMBER
SALAD WITH A
HONEY LIME DRESSING

———

4 LIMES, SLICED AND SEEDED	2 MEDIUM CUCUMBERS
1 CUP HONEY	1 PINT STRAWBERRIES

Combine the lime slices and honey in a food processor, and puree. Wash, peel, seed, and slice the cucumbers. Hull and quarter the strawberries. Combine the cucumbers, strawberries, and dressing; toss gently. Serve.

THREE MUSTARD

VINAIGRETTE

$^1/_3$ CUP WHOLE-GRAIN MUSTARD

$^1/_3$ CUP DIJON MUSTARD

$^1/_3$ CUP SPICY BROWN MUSTARD

$^1/_4$ CUP WORCESTERSHIRE SAUCE

$^1/_2$ CUP GRANULATED SUGAR

1 CUP ICE WATER

5 CUPS SALAD OIL

Combine all of the ingredients except the oil in a mixer or food processor. Turn the machine on, and slowly add the oil until entirely incorporated. Season with salt and pepper. Refrigerate 3 hours before using.

RASPBERRY CHAMBORD

VINAIGRETTE

———

1 TWELVE-OUNCE BAG FROZEN
   RASPBERRIES

2 LARGE EGGS

1/2 CUP GRANULATED SUGAR

1/4 CUP RASPBERRY JAM

3 PINTS SALAD OIL

1 PINT RASPBERRY OR CIDER
   VINEGAR

1/4 CUP CHAMBORD LIQUEUR

In a mixer or food processor combine the thawed raspberries, eggs, sugar, and jam. Turn the machine on, and slowly add the oil until entirely incorporated. Add the vinegar and Chambord. Refrigerate 3 hours before using.

FRUIT SALAD WITH A
LAVENDER HONEY MAYONNAISE

———

1 CUP MAYONNAISE	6 CUPS DICED FRUIT—
1 TABLESPOON MINCED	BLUEBERRIES, STRAWBERRIES,
LAVENDER	GREEN GRAPES,
1/4 CUP HONEY	CANTALOUPE MELONS.
	LETTUCE LEAVES

Blend the mayonnaise, lavender, and honey until smooth. Place
a mixture of seasonal diced fresh fruit and berries on a lettuce-
lined salad plate, and top with a dollop of the lavender honey
mayonnaise.

CABBAGE SALAD WITH A

LAVENDER VINEGAR

---

6 CUPS GREEN CABBAGE

$^2/_3$ CUP OLIVE OIL

$^1/_3$ CUP WHITE WINE VINEGAR

$^1/_3$ CUP GRANULATED SUGAR

2 FRESH LAVENDER SPRIGS

Shred the cabbage in a food processor. Combine the oil, vinegar, sugar, and lavender in a blender, and mix for 30 seconds. Toss the cabbage with the dressing. Season with salt and pepper.

ENTRÉES

One of the great things about not having a national cuisine is that we're not hampered by tradition. It was not traditional to cream radishes and serve them in the center of a spinach ring, or perhaps to serve oysters and sausages in the same dish, or to add rose water to an apple pie. But these Shaker recipes are wonderful evidence that Shaker food was way beyond what the average American was eating in pre–Civil War times.

It was not as if the Shakers had devised a sacred group of recipes that were some mysterious part of their religion. Quite the contrary. Eldress Bertha told me that she remembers as a child that the older Sisters who cooked took recipes from magazines and off the backs of packages, worked them around, and passed them on. They also wrote some of these recipes in longhand in ledgers and changed them as they cooked. Sister Edith Greene, the last black Sister at Canterbury, according to Sister Ethel, left her book of recipes to be passed on and other Sisters subsequently added their own ideas, cutouts, and notations. It's a wonderful book with names for recipes like Acid Biscuits, Bannock, Indian Rolls, and Spider Corn Cakes.

In the preparation of the entrée more than anywhere else in the meal have we taken the most liberties in the names of Shaker cooking. Knowing how advanced the Shakers were in their perception of the necessities of life, I feel confident that if the Village were thriving today with happy, vibrant, interested, and dedicated people, their kitchen would probably be putting out exactly the same kind of food we've written about in this book.

FISH AND SHELLFISH

———

Since these recipes were developed in New England I'll begin with lobster. I found only two Shaker recipes for lobster. One was for thermidor, and the other was for baked and stuffed lobster. Lobster was once so plentiful in New England that in our early history it was actually a crime to feed your prisoners, slaves, and indentured servants lobster more than five times a week. What was once the least valued has now become a luxury. I suppose that's the danger of placing little value on anything. You run the risk of losing it altogether—things like pure water and air; fresh, unradiated fruits and vegetables; and all chemical-free foods.

Canterbury was no more than a day's ride from the coast so one can only assume that fresh fish was available often. There are, in fact, more recipes for scallops in Shaker cookbooks than for any other fish or shellfish. But for a long time Shakers ate meats—beef, pork, and lamb—more than they ate fish. Perhaps this was because they were a hard-working group of people, and fish dinners don't always feel satisfying to people who have spent hours in manual labor. Nonetheless, we feel, considering the conditions today as well as the availability, cost, and taste of seafood, that we should include some of our favorite recipes for fish, including a little lobster.

BAKED SALMON
WITH LOBSTER PÂTÉ IN
AN HERB CREAM SAUCE

SERVES 8

8 FIVE-OUNCE SALMON FILLETS	HERB CREAM SAUCE
LOBSTER PATÉ	

LOBSTER PÂTÉ

½ POUND LOBSTER TAILS, COOKED	1 TABLESPOON MINCED GARLIC
	1 TEASPOON PAPRIKA
1 EGG	JUICE OF 1 LEMON
¼ CUP SLICED SCALLIONS	

Combine pâté ingredients in a food processor, and blend until well mixed (do not overmix), or chop the lobster meat finely by hand and mix with remaining ingredients. Season with salt and pepper. Set aside.

HERB CREAM SAUCE

½ CUP LOBSTER BROTH	2 TABLESPOONS MINCED FRESH
¼ CUP MILK	HERBS OF CHOICE
¾ CUP BUTTERMILK	

Combine sauce ingredients in a sauce pot, and simmer until reduced by half. Season with salt and pepper.

METHOD OF PREPARATION

Place salmon fillets in a buttered baking dish. Use a pastry bag to pipe (or a spoon to spread) the Lobster Pâté onto each salmon fillet. Bake in a 450° F oven for 15–20 minutes. Pour the Herb Cream Sauce over each fillet, and serve.

BAKED SALMON FILLETS WITH PEAS AND ONIONS IN A CREAM SAUCE

SERVES 8

Salmon and peas have long been a New England favorite tradition that the Shakers also observed. We felt we couldn't do less.

| 8 EIGHT-OUNCE SALMON FILLETS | CREAM SAUCE |

CREAM SAUCE

1/2 STICK UNSALTED BUTTER	1 TEASPOON MINT OR
1 TABLESPOON MINCED GARLIC	TARRAGON
1/4 CUP FLOUR	1 CUP GREEN PEAS, COOKED
1 CUP WHITE WINE	1 CUP PEARL ONIONS, COOKED
2 CUPS LIGHT CREAM	

Melt the butter in a saucepan. Sauté the garlic until soft but not brown. Stir in the flour to make a roux. Add the wine and cream, stirring until smooth. Simmer 5–10 minutes. Add the mint or tarragon, peas, and onions. Take 1/2 cup of the sauce, puree in a blender, and return to the remaining sauce. Season with salt and pepper. Set aside.

METHOD OF PREPARATION

Place the salmon fillets in a buttered baking dish. Cover with the Cream Sauce, and bake in a 400° F oven for 20–30 minutes. Serve.

PAN-FRIED SALMON STEAKS

WITH LIME BASIL BUTTER

————

SERVES 6

Most people prefer the West Coast salmon from the Columbia River. Scottish salmon, if you can get it fresh, is a very rare treat. In Maine, salmon is being farmed. Farmed salmon has a very light pink meat, almost white at times, and it is not nearly as large as the West Coast variety. They are, though, very tasty. Salmon simply cleaned, boned as much as possible, dipped in a little egg and flour, and fried in a skillet with some bacon grease is a kind of cooking that has almost disap-peared thanks to the cholesterol paranoia. It is, however, some of the best-tasting cooking you'll ever find, and some of the most basic North American. Here is another way to do almost the same thing.

1/2 STICK UNSALTED BUTTER	GARLIC
1/4 CUP FLOUR	PAPRIKA TO TASTE
6 EIGHT-OUNCE SALMON	BASIL TO TASTE
STEAKS	JUICE OF 1 LIME

In a frying pan melt the butter. Lightly flour the salmon steaks. Place the steaks in the frying pan over medium heat, and cook 4–5 minutes on each side. Season each side of the steaks with salt, pepper, garlic, paprika, and basil. When you flip the steaks to cook the second side, add the freshly squeezed lime juice. Place cooked salmon steaks on a serving tray, and pour pan drippings over them. Serve immediately.

BAKED SALMON FILLETS IN A

BACON POTATO CREAM SAUCE

SERVES 8

Sister Ethel often speaks of one of her favorite dishes, Baked Potato with Creamed Salmon. That dish is one of the first recipes that involved canned fish. It basically is a baked potato split open, slathered with butter, and deluged in a sauce of thickened milk or light cream seasoned with salt and pepper and mixed into canned salmon. Sister Ethel describes it, "Why, it's very simple, yes, you just bake a potato, and then you make a lovely white sauce and add a can of salmon and a little salt and pepper. Yes, and you must put some butter on the potato and then the creamed salmon. Oh, that was so good in the winter when you'd come in from the cold."

Once I came by to visit when she was eating her supper, a piece of brown bread covered with baked beans and a dollop of catsup. Do you have any idea how old-fashioned that meal is? There are even foods from my childhood that don't, or almost don't, appear anymore on a dinner table. Barley, kohlrabi, kidneys, blue Hubbard squash, and cranberry beans are just a few. I'm certain there are many more. Think of the foods in your childhood. Their disappearance has to do with the homogenization of the North American culture. The more American we become, the further we are from our ethnicity. Fourth-generation Italians, Swedes, and Poles are more likely to be eating string beans, carrots, and corn than garbanzo beans, lingonberries, or blood sausage. In the interest of old-fashioned ways, and Sister Ethel, we came up with the following recipe.

8 EIGHT-OUNCE SALMON	BACON POTATO CREAM SAUCE
FILLETS	

BACON POTATO CREAM SAUCE

¼ STICK UNSALTED BUTTER	3 TABLESPOONS MINCED CHIVES
2 TABLESPOONS MINCED	½ CUP BACON BITS, COOKED
ONIONS	HEAVY CREAM TO COVER
1 MEDIUM POTATO, PEELED	MILK TO COVER
AND SHREDDED	

Melt the butter in a saucepan, and sauté the onions. Add the shredded potato, chives, bacon, and equal amounts of heavy cream and milk to cover the mixture. Simmer the sauce 10–15 minutes until the potatoes are soft. Season sauce with salt and pepper, and keep warm.

METHOD OF PREPARATION

Place the salmon fillets in a buttered baking dish. Bake in a 450°F oven for 12–15 minutes or until cooked. Pour the sauce over each fillet and serve.

BAKED SEA SCALLOPS IN A

CIDER SOUR CREAM SAUCE

SERVES 4

2 POUNDS SEA SCALLOPS	2 TABLESPOONS UNSALTED
CIDER SOUR CREAM SAUCE	BUTTER, MELTED
1 CUP BREAD CRUMBS	

CIDER SOUR CREAM SAUCE

2 TABLESPOONS UNSALTED	$1/2$ CUP WHITE WINE
BUTTER	$1/4$ CUP DIJON MUSTARD
2 TABLESPOONS MINCED	1 CUP APPLE JUICE
SHALLOTS	CONCENTRATE
3 TABLESPOONS FLOUR	3 CUPS SOUR CREAM

Melt the butter in a saucepan, and sauté the shallots. Add the flour, and stir to make a roux. Add the wine, mustard, and apple juice concentrate, stirring until smooth. Add the sour cream, and cook over very low heat for 10–15 minutes. Season with salt and pepper. Set aside.

METHOD OF PREPARATION

Place the sea scallops in a buttered baking dish. Pour the Cider Sour Cream Sauce over the scallops. Mix the bread crumbs with the melted butter. Sprinkle the scallops with the buttered bread crumbs. Bake in a 400° F oven for 30 minutes or until bubbly and lightly browned. Serve.

SEA SCALLOPS BAKED IN A

GINGER APPLE BUTTER

SERVES 8

2 POUNDS SEA SCALLOPS | GINGER APPLE BUTTER

GINGER APPLE BUTTER

2 CUPS APPLE BUTTER

1/4 CUP SHERRY

JUICE OF 1 LEMON

1 TABLESPOON FRESHLY GRATED

GINGER ROOT

2 TABLESPOONS HERBS DE

PROVENCE

Combine the apple butter, sherry, lemon juice, grated ginger, and herbs in a saucepan and warm. Season the sauce with salt and pepper.

METHOD OF PREPARATION

Place the sea scallops in a baking dish. Pour the warm Ginger Apple Butter over the scallops. Bake in a 500° F oven for 15 minutes or until cooked. Serve.

SEA SCALLOPS FRICASSEE

WITH LOBSTER

SAFFRON CREAM SAUCE

SERVES 4–6

2 POUNDS SEA SCALLOPS	3/4 CUP FLOUR
2 EGGS	1/2 CUP OLIVE OIL
1 CUP MILK	LOBSTER SAFFRON CREAM
1/4 CUP CORNMEAL	SAUCE

LOBSTER SAFFRON CREAM SAUCE

1 CUP LOBSTER MEAT, COOKED	1 CUP HEAVY CREAM
1 EGG	1/8 TEASPOON SAFFRON
1 CUP MILK	1/2 TEASPOON PAPRIKA

Combine the sauce ingredients in a blender, and puree. Season with salt and pepper. Set aside.

METHOD OF PREPARATION

Remove the muscles from the scallops. Beat the eggs and milk together. Coat the scallops in the egg wash. Mix cornmeal and flour. Coat the scallops in the flour mixture. Heat a frying pan with the olive oil until very hot. Add the scallops, and cook until browned. Remove from pan, and dry on paper towels. Place the scallops in a baking dish. Cover the scallops with the Lobster Saffron Cream Sauce. Bake in 450° F oven 12–15 minutes. Serve.

CATFISH FILLETS PAN-FRIED IN MAYONNAISE WITH LEMON HERB CUSTARD SAUCE

―――――

SERVES 8

There are two kinds of readily available catfish that I can recall. One of them is from the Mississippi River: enormous fish weighing fifty to eighty pounds, and it tastes terrific. Smaller varieties of catfish are found in lesser rivers, ponds, and small lakes. And, along with this smaller variety, there is an even smaller group known as bullheads. Ugly to look at, they can also spike you if you're not careful. To make matters more interesting, particularly for the very young fisherman, they usually swallow the hook all the way to their tail. It's always a pleasure trying to retrieve it. If you're not fishing, then keep an eye open for catfish in your local fish market and buy whichever variety you can. Catfish is oily, has a great texture, lots of protein and, if you like fish, this must not be missed.

LEMON HERB CUSTARD SAUCE

PAN DRIPPINGS	JUICE OF 2 LEMONS
1 STICK UNSALTED BUTTER, MELTED	1 TEASPOON MINCED GARLIC
4 EGGS, BEATEN	1 TABLESPOON MINCED TARRAGON

In the frying pan whisk the pan drippings (from frying the catfish) together with the butter, eggs, lemon juice, garlic, and tarragon. Cook over very low heat until the mixture thickens. Whip the sauce in a blender until smooth. Season with salt and pepper.

METHOD OF PREPARATION

8 EIGHT-OUNCE CATFISH FILLETS	GARLIC
	PARSLEY
3/4 CUP FLOUR	TARRAGON
1/4 CUP MAYONNAISE	JUICE OF 1 LEMON

Lightly coat the catfish fillets with the flour. Puree the mayonnaise in a blender until smooth. Melt the mayonnaise in a frying pan over medium heat. Add the fillets, sprinkle with the garlic, parsley, and tarragon, and season with salt and pepper. Cook 4–5 minutes. Add the lemon juice when you flip the fillets to cook the other side 4–5 minutes. Remove fillets from pan. Save some of the drippings for the sauce. Pour the sauce over each cooked catfish fillet and serve.

BAKED FILLETS OF TURBOT IN
A SORREL CREAM SAUCE

SERVES 8

SORREL CREAM SAUCE

¹/₂ STICK UNSALTED BUTTER

1 TABLESPOON MINCED

    SHALLOTS

1 TABLESPOON MINCED GARLIC

¹/₄ CUP FLOUR

1 CUP MINCED FRESH SORREL

1 CUP WHITE WINE OR SHERRY

2 CUPS LIGHT CREAM

8 EIGHT-TO-TEN-OUNCE

    TURBOT FILLETS

In a saucepan melt the butter, and sauté the shallots and garlic 2–3 minutes. Add the flour, and stir to make a roux. Add the sorrel, wine or sherry, and cream, stirring until smooth. Simmer the sauce for 5–10 minutes. Season with salt and pepper. Set aside.

METHOD OF PREPARATION

Place the turbot fillets in a baking dish. Pour the Sorrel Cream Sauce over the fillets. Bake in a 450° F oven for 15–20 minutes. Serve.

BAKED TURBOT FILLETS STUFFED
WITH CINNAMON APRICOTS
IN A CIDER SOUR CREAM SAUCE

SERVES 8

8 SIX-TO-EIGHT-OUNCE	CINNAMON APRICOT STUFFING
TURBOT FILLETS	CIDER SOUR CREAM SAUCE

CINNAMON APRICOT
STUFFING

1 POUND APRICOTS, PITTED	JUICE OF 1 LEMON
AND SLICED	1/2 CUP FRESH BREAD CRUMBS
2 EGGS, BEATEN	1 TEASPOON CINNAMON
1/4 CUP WHITE WINE	

Combine stuffing ingredients in a mixing bowl, and mix well by hand. Season with salt and pepper. Set aside.

CIDER SOUR CREAM SAUCE

2 TABLESPOONS UNSALTED	1 CUP HARD CIDER
BUTTER	2 CUPS SOUR CREAM
3 TABLESPOONS FLOUR	

Melt the butter in a saucepan. Stir in the flour to make a roux. Add the hard cider, stirring until smooth. Add the sour cream, stirring until smooth. Cook the sauce over very low heat for 5–10 minutes. Season with salt and pepper. Set aside.

METHOD OF PREPARATION

Divide the Cinnamon Apricot Stuffing among the turbot fillets. Roll up the stuffing in each fillet, and place in a buttered baking dish. Cover the fillets with the Cider Sour Cream Sauce. Bake in a 400° F oven for 30 minutes or until cooked. Serve.

BAKED DOVER SOLE FILLETS WITH TOASTED HAZELNUTS IN A FRANGELICO PEACH SAUCE

SERVES 8

8 SIX-TO-EIGHT-OUNCE DOVER
SOLE FILLETS

FRANGELICO PEACH SAUCE

FRANGELICO PEACH SAUCE

2 PEACHES, PITTED AND SLICED

1/2 STICK UNSALTED BUTTER,
   MELTED

1 CUP CREAM CHEESE

1 EGG

1/4 CUP FRANGELICO LIQUEUR

1 TABLESPOON FLOUR

3/4 CUP TOASTED CHOPPED
   HAZELNUTS

Combine the sliced peaches, melted butter, cream cheese, egg, liqueur, and flour in a blender, and mix until smooth. Pour the sauce into a saucepan. Add the hazelnuts, and simmer sauce 5–10 minutes. Season with salt and pepper. Set aside.

METHOD OF PREPARATION

Place the Dover sole fillets in a buttered baking dish. Pour the Frangelico Peach Sauce over the fillets. Bake in a 450° F oven for 15–20 minutes. Serve.

BAKED GRAY SOLE IN

A LOBSTER NASTURTIUM

CREAM SAUCE

————

SERVES 6

| 3–4 POUNDS GRAY SOLE | LOBSTER NASTURTIUM CREAM |
| FILLETS | SAUCE |

LOBSTER NASTURTIUM
CREAM SAUCE

1/2 STICK UNSALTED BUTTER	15 NASTURTIUM BLOSSOMS
1/4 CUP FLOUR	1 CUP CHOPPED COOKED
3/4 CUP WHITE WINE	LOBSTER MEAT
2 1/2 CUPS LIGHT CREAM	

Melt the butter in a saucepan. Add the flour, and stir to make a roux. Add the wine, and stir until smooth. Add the light cream, and stir until smooth. Add the nasturtium blossoms and chopped lobster meat. Simmer the sauce over low heat for 7–10 minutes. Season with salt and pepper. Puree the sauce in a blender until smooth. Set aside.

METHOD OF PREPARATION

Place the gray sole fillets in a baking dish. Pour the Lobster Nasturtium Cream Sauce over the fillets. Bake in a 450° F oven for 15–20 minutes or until cooked. Serve.

BAKED SOLE WITH SALMON STUFFING
AND A CIDER HOLLANDAISE SAUCE

SERVES 8

8 SIX-TO-EIGHT-OUNCE SOLE

    FILLETS

SALMON STUFFING OF CHOICE

½ CUP WATER

CIDER HOLLANDAISE SAUCE

SALMON STUFFING 1

1 POUND SALMON, CUT INTO

    HALF-INCH CUBES

2 EGGS

½ CUP HEAVY CREAM

½ STICK UNSALTED BUTTER,

    MELTED

JUICE OF 1 LEMON

1 TABLESPOON LOBSTER

    BOUILLON

1 TABLESPOON MINCED GARLIC

2 TABLESPOONS CHOPPED

    PARSLEY

Combine the stuffing ingredients in a bowl, and mix by hand.
Season with salt and pepper. Set aside.

SALMON STUFFING 2

¾ POUND SALMON FILLET

½ POUND SCALLOPS

2 EGGS, BEATEN

½ CUP HEAVY CREAM

½ STICK UNSALTED BUTTER,

    MELTED

JUICE OF 1 LEMON

1 CUP GRATED CHEDDAR CHEESE

1 CUP GRATED SWISS CHEESE

2 TABLESPOONS CHOPPED

    PARSLEY

Cube the salmon fillet into half-inch pieces. Combine stuffing ingredients in a bowl, and mix by hand. Season with salt and pepper. Set aside.

CIDER HOLLANDAISE SAUCE

4 EGGS	JUICE OF 1 LEMON
2 STICKS UNSALTED BUTTER	1 TEASPOON MINCED GARLIC
1/4 CUP APPLE CIDER OR APPLE	
JUICE CONCENTRATE	

Combine all ingredients in a double boiler, and whisk constantly over low heat until the sauce thickens. Whip the sauce in a blender until smooth. Season with salt and pepper. Set aside.

METHOD OF PREPARATION

Divide the Salmon Stuffing of your choice among the sole fillets. Roll up the fillets. Place the stuffed fillets in a baking dish. Add the water to the baking dish to keep the fish moist. Bake in a 450° F oven for 15–20 minutes or until cooked. Pour the Cider Hollandaise Sauce over the fillets, and serve.

BAKED FILLETS OF SOLE STUFFED WITH AN APPLE SHRIMP PÂTÉ IN A LOBSTER CREAM SAUCE

SERVES 8

8 SIX-TO-EIGHT-OUNCE SOLE FILLETS	APPLE SHRIMP PÂTÉ LOBSTER CREAM SAUCE

APPLE SHRIMP PÂTÉ

1 POUND RAW SHRIMP	2 SLICES OF BREAD, CRUST
2 APPLES, CORED	REMOVED
1/4 CUP SLICED SCALLIONS	1 EGG
	JUICE OF 1 LEMON

Peel and devein the shrimp, then rinse under cold water. Place all the ingredients in a food processor, and grind until just before the pâté turns into a paste. Season with salt and pepper. Set aside.

LOBSTER CREAM SAUCE

½ STICK UNSALTED BUTTER	3 CUPS LIGHT CREAM
¼ CUP FLOUR	1 CUP DICED COOKED LOBSTER
2 TABLESPOONS APPLE BRANDY	MEAT

Melt the butter in a saucepan. Stir in the flour to make a roux. Stir in the apple brandy and light cream until smooth. Simmer the sauce for 7–10 minutes over low heat, stirring occasionally. Add the diced lobster meat. Season with salt and pepper. Set aside.

METHOD OF PREPARATION

Divide the Apple Shrimp Pâté among the sole fillets, and roll them up with the pâté inside. Place the fillets in a baking dish. Bake in a 450° F oven for 15–20 minutes or until cooked. Pour the Lobster Cream Sauce evenly over the baked fillets, and serve.

BAKED FILLETS OF SOLE IN A

SALMON BUTTERMILK SAUCE

SERVES 8

½ STICK UNSALTED BUTTER	1 POUND SALMON FILLETS, CUT
¼ CUP FLOUR	IN HALF-INCH CUBES
¾ CUP WHITE WINE OR SHERRY	8 SIX-TO-EIGHT-OUNCE SOLE
1 CUP BUTTERMILK	FILLETS
1 CUP LIGHT CREAM	

Melt the butter in a saucepan. Add the flour, and stir to make a roux. Add the wine or sherry, and stir until smooth. Add the buttermilk and light cream, and stir until smooth. Add the cubed salmon, and simmer the sauce over low heat for 10–15 minutes. Season with salt and pepper. Set aside.

METHOD OF PREPARATION

Place the sole fillets in a buttered baking dish. Pour the Salmon Buttermilk Sauce over the fillets. Bake in a 450° F oven for 12–15 minutes or until cooked. Serve.

FILLETS OF COD WITH SALMON MOUSSE BAKED IN A CIDER BUTTER

SERVES 8

8 FIVE-TO-SIX-OUNCE COD FILLETS	SALMON MOUSSE CIDER BUTTER

SALMON MOUSSE

1 POUND SALMON FILLETS	JUICE OF 1/2 LEMON
1 CUP HEAVY CREAM	

Puree the salmon fillets in a food processor. Add the cream, blending until smooth. Add the lemon juice. Season with salt and pepper. Set aside.

CIDER BUTTER

1/2 STICK UNSALTED BUTTER	1/2 CUP HARD CIDER OR APPLE JUICE CONCENTRATE

Combine the butter and cider or apple juice concentrate in a saucepan. Bring the sauce to a boil. Set aside.

METHOD OF PREPARATION

Place the cod fillets in a baking dish. Use a pastry bag to pipe (or a spoon to spread) the mousse on top of each fillet. Pour the Cider Butter over each fillet. Bake in 450° F oven for 15–20 minutes or until cooked. Serve.

BAKED SEAFOOD CASSEROLE IN A GINGER CIDER SOUR CREAM SAUCE

SERVES 6

2–3 POUNDS FRESH SEAFOOD:

   1 POUND SCALLOPS

   1 POUND SHRIMP

   1/2 POUND LOBSTER MEAT

1/2 POUND WHITEFISH

GINGER CIDER SOUR CREAM SAUCE

SEASONED BREAD CRUMBS

GINGER CIDER SOUR CREAM SAUCE

2 TABLESPOONS UNSALTED

   BUTTER

1/4 CUP LEEKS, WASHED AND

   SLICED

3 TABLESPOONS FLOUR

1 CUP CIDER OR APPLE JUICE

   CONCENTRATE

2 CUPS SOUR CREAM

1 TABLESPOON CHOPPED

   PARSLEY

1 TABLESPOON CHOPPED

   GINGER

Melt the butter in a saucepan and sauté the leeks. Add the flour, and stir to make a roux. Add the cider or apple juice concentrate, and stir until smooth. Stir in the sour cream, parsley, and ginger, and simmer 5–10 minutes. Season with salt and pepper. Set aside.

SEASONED BREAD CRUMBS

1 CUP BREAD CRUMBS	2 TEASPOONS LEMON JUICE
¼ CUP GRATED CHEDDAR	2 TABLESPOONS UNSALTED
CHEESE	BUTTER, MELTED

Combine the bread crumbs and cheese. Moisten with the lemon juice and melted butter. Season with salt and pepper. Set aside.

METHOD OF PREPARATION

Place the fresh seafood in a 2-quart casserole dish. Pour the Ginger Cider Sour Cream Sauce over the seafood. Top the casserole with the Seasoned Bread Crumbs. Bake in a 450° F over for 15–20 minutes or until cooked. Serve.

CURRIED SWORDFISH WITH
TOASTED ALMONDS AND COCONUT

SERVES 6

3–4 POUNDS FRESH	½ CUP SLIVERED ALMONDS
SWORDFISH	¼ CUP UNSWEETENED
CURRY SAUCE	COCONUT FLAKES

CURRY SAUCE

½ STICK UNSALTED BUTTER	2 CUPS BUTTERMILK
¼ CUP FLOUR	2 TABLESPOONS CURRY POWDER
1 CUP FISH STOCK OR CHICKEN	
STOCK	

In a saucepan melt the butter, and blend in the flour to make a roux. Stir in the stock until smooth. Add the buttermilk and curry powder, stirring until smooth. Simmer the sauce 7–10 minutes over low heat, stirring often. Season with salt and pepper. Set aside.

METHOD OF PREPARATION

Cut the swordfish into 1-inch cubes. Place the swordfish in a baking dish, and toss with the Curry Sauce. Top the fish with the slivered almonds and coconut flakes. Bake in a 450° F oven for 15–20 minutes or until cooked. Serve.

BIRDS

————

DUCK

It was surprising to see that there was not a lot of evidence for duck, goose, and wild bird recipes in Shaker recipe books. It might be because it was simpler to raise chickens and turkeys than to hunt for dinner. Had the Shakers eaten more duck, they might have come up with the following.

ROASTING A DUCKLING

————

Duckling is not easily carved, so I advise you to have your local butcher cut the ducks in half for you. Purchase 4^1/2–5 pound ducks, and allow half a duck per person.

> Preheat the oven to 350° F. Place the duck halves on a raised rack inside of a roasting pan. Pierce the skins of the ducks with a fork. This helps to release the fat during cooking. Season the ducks with kosher salt, pepper, and rosemary. Place in the oven, and roast 1 hour for medium doneness or 1^1/2 hours for well done. Glaze the ducks the last 15 minutes of roasting, or you may serve the sauce on the side if you wish.

GINGER CIDER

ROAST DUCKLING

---

1 CUP CIDER OR APPLE JUICE
CONCENTRATE

1 CUP RED WINE

2 MEDIUM APPLES, SLICED

¼ CUP DIJON MUSTARD

1–2 TABLESPOONS GRATED
GINGER

Prepare the Roast Duckling. (See p. 75.) Simmer sauce
ingredients in a saucepan until reduced by half. Glaze the ducks.
Serve.

ROAST DUCKLING WITH

RASPBERRY MAPLE SAUCE

———

3 CUPS FRESH RASPBERRIES	¼ CUP TEQUILA
2 CUPS MAPLE SYRUP	4 TABLESPOONS DIJON
2 TABLESPOONS LEMON JUICE	MUSTARD

Prepare the Roast Duckling. (See p. 75.) In a blender puree 1 cup of the raspberries with the maple syrup, lemon juice, tequila, and mustard. Pour the sauce into a saucepan, and simmer until reduced by half. Add remaining 2 cups of raspberries.

ROAST DUCKLING IN A
BLUEBERRY LEMONADE SAUCE

―――――

4 LEMONS, SLICED AND SEEDED

2 CUPS GRANULATED SUGAR

2 CUPS WHITE WINE

1 PINT FRESH BLUEBERRIES, PICKED
OVER AND WASHED

Prepare the Roast Duckling. (See p. 75.) Combine the lemon slices, sugar, and wine in a sauce pot, and simmer until reduced by one-third (lemons should be soft). Add the blueberries, and simmer for 5–7 minutes. Glaze the ducks. Serve.

ROAST DUCKLING WITH

HONEYED CRAB APPLE SAUCE

---

¹/₂ POUND CRAB APPLES

2 CUPS RED WINE

1 CUP GRANULATED SUGAR

¹/₂ CUP HONEY

1 TABLESPOON CINNAMON

Prepare the Roast Duckling. (See p. 75.) Combine sauce ingredients in a saucepan, and simmer until the apples become soft. Pour the sauce over the roasted ducks. Serve.

GRILLING DUCK BREASTS

———

Duck breasts are usually available frozen in most supermarkets today. They are as simple to grill as steaks and add a wonderful change of pace to the traditional backyard barbecue.

Defrost the duck breasts according to package instructions. Trim off excess fat. Grill like a steak, but remember that duck breasts cook a little faster than steaks. Baste with any of the above sauces while grilling, or serve a sauce on the side.

CHICKEN

The Shakers raised and dressed out their own chickens, as did almost every rural resident of the United States since the first chickens were cooped. Oddly enough, we didn't find chicken recipes that we thought were completely unique in terms of Shaker cookery. We did find great chicken pot-pie, fried chicken, boiled (stewed) chicken, and roasted chicken. But the recipes always included the entire chicken. Naturally, before refrigeration and freezing, if you killed a bird you figured out a way to eat the entire thing since adequate storage was not available.

Today, however, we can get just breasts, wings, thighs, livers, or drumsticks. Chicken wings, once considered one of the least choice parts of the bird, have now become a national pastime when it comes to snacking. Following are some of the uses we found for this bird of paradise.

BREAST OF CHICKEN STUFFED WITH DUCK AND PEAR PÂTÉ IN A SHIITAKE MUSHROOM SAUCE

SERVES 8

8 EIGHT-OUNCE BONELESS CHICKEN BREASTS, WITH SKIN

DUCK AND PEAR PÂTÉ

PAPRIKA TO TASTE

GARLIC POWDER TO TASTE

CHOPPED PARSLEY TO TASTE

WHITE WINE

DUCK AND PEAR PÂTÉ

1½ POUNDS BONELESS DUCK MEAT

1½ CUPS GRATED JARLSBERG CHEESE

1 TEASPOON THYME

2 TABLESPOONS MINCED GARLIC

1 EGG

½ MEDIUM RED ONION, DICED

2 TABLESPOONS COGNAC

1 MEDIUM PEAR, CORED AND QUARTERED

Combine pâté ingredients in a food processor, and coarsely chop the mixture. Season with salt and pepper. Chill until ready to use.

METHOD OF PREPARATION

Lightly pound the chicken breasts, leaving the skin on. Divide the pâté among the chicken breasts, and stuff them. Place the chicken breasts in a baking dish, and sprinkle with the paprika, granular garlic, and chopped parsley. Season with salt and pepper. Fill the baking dish half an inch deep with white wine. Bake in a 400° F oven for 30–45 minutes or until cooked. Serve with sauce.

SHIITAKE MUSHROOM SAUCE

PAN DRIPPINGS	2–3 CUPS SLICED SHIITAKE
RED WINE	MUSHROOMS

Into a saucepan drain off the pan drippings from baking the chicken. Add an equal amount of red wine. Add the shiitake mushrooms, and simmer for 20–30 minutes over low heat. Season with salt and pepper. Serve over roasted chicken breasts.

OPTIONAL: You may thicken the sauce with flour if desired.

BREAST OF CHICKEN WITH DRIED APPLE BACON STUFFING WITH A RED WINE CIDER GLAZE

SERVES 8

8 EIGHT-OUNCE BONELESS CHICKEN BREASTS, WITH SKIN	PAPRIKA TO TASTE
	GARLIC POWDER TO TASTE
	CHOPPED PARSLEY TO TASTE
DRIED APPLE BACON STUFFING	RED WINE CIDER GLAZE

DRIED APPLE BACON STUFFING

2 CUPS DRIED APPLES, CHOPPED	1/4 CUP SLICED SCALLIONS
2 CUPS BACON BITS, COOKED	1 TABLESPOON MINCED GARLIC
2 EGGS, BEATEN	2 TEASPOONS GRATED GINGER
1/4 CUP WHITE WINE	

Combine all stuffing ingredients in a mixing bowl, and mix well by hand. Season with salt and pepper. Set aside.

RED WINE CIDER GLAZE

| 2 CUPS APPLE JUICE | 2 CUPS RED WINE |
| CONCENTRATE | 1/2 CUP DIJON MUSTARD |

Combine glaze ingredients in a saucepan. Simmer until reduced by half. Set aside.

METHOD OF PREPARATION

Lightly pound the chicken breasts, leaving the skin on. Divide the Dried Apple Bacon Stuffing among the breasts, and stuff. Place the chicken breasts in a roasting pan, and season with salt, pepper, granular garlic, paprika, and chopped parsley. Roast in a 400° F oven for 30–40 minutes or until cooked. Glaze the roasted chicken breasts with the Red Wine Cider Glaze. Serve.

BREAST OF CHICKEN WITH
A BACON SHIITAKE MUSHROOM
STUFFING IN A NATURAL SAUCE

SERVES 8

8 EIGHT-OUNCE BONELESS
CHICKEN BREASTS, WITH
SKIN

BACON SHIITAKE STUFFING

PAPRIKA TO TASTE

GARLIC POWDER TO TASTE

CHOPPED PARSLEY TO TASTE

WHITE WINE

PAN GRAVY

BACON SHIITAKE STUFFING

1 CUP BACON BITS, COOKED

2 CUPS CHOPPED SHIITAKE
MUSHROOMS

1/2 CUP WHITE WINE

2 EGGS, BEATEN

2 TABLESPOONS WARM BACON
GREASE

2 TABLESPOONS MINCED GARLIC

2 TABLESPOONS MINCED FRESH
HERBS OF CHOICE

Combine all stuffing ingredients in a mixing bowl, and mix well
by hand. Season with salt and pepper. Set aside.

METHOD OF PREPARATION

Lightly pound the chicken breasts, leaving the skin on. Divide the Bacon Shiitake Stuffing among the chicken breasts, and roll them up. Place the chicken breasts in a roasting pan, and season with salt, pepper, garlic, paprika, and chopped parsley. Fill the roasting pan half an inch deep with white wine. Roast in a 400° F oven for 30–40 minutes or until cooked.

NATURAL SAUCE

2 CUPS PAN DRIPPINGS	1 EGG
1 TABLESPOON FLOUR	

If lacking full amount of pan drippings, make up the difference with chicken stock or white wine. Combine the pan drippings, flour, and egg in a blender, and mix for 30 seconds. Pour the sauce into a saucepan, and simmer 5–7 minutes. Season with salt and pepper. Pour the sauce over the roasted chicken breasts. Serve.

BREAST OF CHICKEN WITH
A BACON CORNBREAD STUFFING
IN AN ORANGE RHUBARB SAUCE

SERVES 8

8 EIGHT-OUNCE BONELESS
    CHICKEN BREASTS, WITH
    SKIN
BACON CORNBREAD STUFFING

PAPRIKA TO TASTE
GARLIC POWDER TO TASTE
CHOPPED PARSLEY TO TASTE
ORANGE RHUBARB SAUCE

BACON CORNBREAD STUFFING

1 CUP WATER
1 CHICKEN BOUILLON CUBE
1 STICK UNSALTED BUTTER
1 POUND CORNBREAD CRUMBS

2 CUPS BACON BITS, COOKED
2 TABLESPOONS HERBS DE
    PROVENCE

Bring the water, bouillon, and butter to a boil. Stir the hot liquid into a bowl with the cornbread crumbs, bacon bits, and herbs de Provence. Season with salt and pepper. Set aside.

ORANGE RHUBARB SAUCE

2 CUPS RHUBARB, DICED

1 ORANGE, SLICED AND SEEDED

1 CUP GRANULATED SUGAR

2 CUPS WHITE WINE

2 CUPS WATER

Combine all ingredients in a saucepan. Simmer the mixture until the orange slices become soft. Puree in a blender until smooth. Set aside. Serve.

METHOD OF PREPARATION

Lightly pound the chicken breasts, leaving the skin on. Divide the Bacon Cornbread Stuffing among the chicken breasts and stuff. Place in a baking pan and season with salt, pepper, granular garlic, paprika, and chopped parsley. Roast in a 400° F oven for 30–40 minutes or until cooked. Glaze the chicken with the Orange Rhubarb Sauce, and serve.

BREAST OF CHICKEN WITH A BACON STUFFING IN A RED WINE RHUBARB SAUCE

SERVES 8

8 EIGHT-OUNCE BONELESS CHICKEN BREASTS, WITH SKIN

BACON STUFFING

PAPRIKA TO TASTE

GARLIC POWDER TO TASTE

CHOPPED PARSLEY TO TASTE

RED WINE RHUBARB SAUCE

BACON STUFFING

3 CUPS BACON BITS, COOKED

1 MEDIUM ONION, DICED

1 CUP DICED CELERY

2 EGGS, BEATEN

1 TABLESPOON MINCED BASIL

1 TABLESPOON MINCED SAGE

1 TABLESPOON MINCED GARLIC

1/2 CUP BREAD CRUMBS

Combine all stuffing ingredients in a mixing bowl and mix well by hand. Season with salt and pepper. Set aside.

RED WINE RHUBARB SAUCE

2 CUPS DICED RHUBARB	2 CUPS GRANULATED SUGAR
1 CUP RED WINE	½ CUP DIJON MUSTARD

Combine sauce ingredients in a saucepan. Simmer until the rhubarb is soft. Puree in a blender until smooth. Set aside.

METHOD OF PREPARATION

Lightly pound the chicken breasts, leaving the skin on. Divide the Bacon Stuffing among the chicken breasts, and stuff. Place in a baking pan and season with salt, pepper, granular garlic, paprika, and chopped parsley. Roast in a 400° F oven for 30–40 minutes or until cooked. Glaze with the Red Wine Rhubarb Sauce. Serve.

BREAST OF CHICKEN WITH LOBSTER IN A SWEET AND SOUR GLAZE

SERVES 8

4 ONE-POUND BONE-IN	CHOPPED PARSLEY TO TASTE
CHICKEN BREASTS	2 CUPS COOKED LOBSTER BODY
PAPRIKA TO TASTE	MEAT
GARLIC POWDER TO TASTE	SWEET AND SOUR GLAZE

SWEET AND SOUR GLAZE

1 CUP MAPLE SYRUP	4 TABLESPOONS CIDER VINEGAR
1 CUP APPLE JUICE	1/2 CUP DIJON MUSTARD
CONCENTRATE	JUICE OF 1 LEMON

Combine all glaze ingredients in a saucepan. Simmer until reduced by one-third. Set aside.

METHOD OF PREPARATION

Place the chicken breasts in a roasting pan. Season the chicken breasts with salt, pepper, granular garlic, paprika, and chopped parsley. Roast in a 400° F oven for 30–40 minutes or until cooked. When cool enough to handle, skin the chicken breast, remove the meat from the bones, and place in a baking dish. Add the lobster body meat. Cover the chicken and lobster with the Sweet and Sour Glaze. Bake in a 450° F oven for 10–12 minutes (cook only until heated; be careful not to overcook).

BREAST OF CHICKEN IN A SORREL

SHIITAKE MUSHROOM SAUCE

SERVES 8

4 ONE-POUND BONE-IN

CHICKEN BREASTS

PAPRIKA TO TASTE

GARLIC POWDER TO TASTE

CHOPPED PARSLEY TO TASTE

SORREL SHIITAKE MUSHROOM

SAUCE

SORREL SHIITAKE MUSHROOM SAUCE

1 STICK UNSALTED

BUTTER

2 TABLESPOONS MINCED

SHALLOTS

2 TABLESPOONS MINCED

GARLIC

2 CUPS SLICED SHIITAKE

MUSHROOMS

1/2 CUP FLOUR

1 CUP WHITE WINE

2 CUPS CHICKEN STOCK

2 CUPS CHOPPED SORREL

1 CUP HEAVY CREAM

Melt the butter in a saucepan, and cook the shallots and garlic 2–3 minutes. Add the sliced mushrooms, and cook until soft. Stir in the flour to form a paste. Add the wine and stock, stirring until smooth. Add the chopped sorrel. Simmer the sauce 10–15 minutes. Add the cream. Season with salt and pepper. Set aside.

METHOD OF PREPARATION

Rinse the chicken breasts under cold water and pat dry. Split the chicken breasts in half with a French knife. Place the breasts in a roasting pan. Season with salt, pepper, granular garlic, paprika, and chopped parsley. Roast in a 400° F oven for 30–40 minutes or until cooked. Pour the Shiitake Mushroom Sauce over the roasted chicken breasts. Serve.

BREAST OF CHICKEN WITH CHICKEN LIVER STUFFING AND COUNTRY-STYLE CREAM GRAVY

SERVES 8

8 EIGHT-OUNCE BONELESS CHICKEN BREASTS	GARLIC POWDER TO TASTE
CHICKEN LIVER STUFFING	CHOPPED PARSLEY TO TASTE
PAPRIKA TO TASTE	COUNTRY-STYLE CREAM GRAVY

CHICKEN LIVER STUFFING

¼ CUP BACON GREASE	1 TABLESPOON MINCED GARLIC
1 POUND CHICKEN LIVERS	1 TABLESPOON THYME OR
1 EGG, BEATEN	ROSEMARY
1 CUP FRESH BREAD CRUMBS	

Heat bacon grease in a frying pan, and sauté the chicken livers. Reserve the frying pan and drippings for gravy. Combine the cooked chicken livers with the remaining stuffing ingredients in a food processor, and chop only until all ingredients are mixed well. Season with salt and pepper. Set aside.

COUNTRY-STYLE CREAM GRAVY

PAN DRIPPINGS	1–1½ CUPS MILK
3 TABLESPOONS FLOUR	

In the frying pan you cooked the chicken livers in, add the flour, and stir to form a paste. Stir in the milk and cook over low heat until the milk thickens. Season with salt and pepper. Set aside.

METHOD OF PREPARATION

Lightly pound the chicken breasts. Divide the Chicken Liver Stuffing among the chicken breasts, and stuff. Place in a baking pan and season with salt, pepper, granular garlic, paprika, and chopped parsley. Roast in a 400° F oven for 30–40 minutes or until cooked. Pour the Country-Style Cream Gravy over the chicken breasts. Serve.

BREAST OF CHICKEN WITH OLD-FASHIONED SAGE DRESSING AND CRANBERRY MAPLE GLAZE

SERVES 8

8 EIGHT-OUNCE BONELESS
CHICKEN BREASTS,
WITH SKIN
OLD-FASHIONED SAGE DRESSING

PAPRIKA TO TASTE
GARLIC POWDER TO TASTE
CHOPPED PARSLEY TO TASTE
CRANBERRY MAPLE GLAZE

OLD-FASHIONED SAGE DRESSING

½ LOAF BREAD, SLICED
⅓ CUP WARM BACON GREASE
⅔ CUP BUTTERMILK

1 CUP DICED CELERY
1 MEDIUM ONION, MINCED
3 TABLESPOONS MINCED SAGE

Place the slices of bread in an oven and toast. In a mixing bowl crumble the toasted bread. Add the remaining ingredients, and mix well by hand. Season with salt and pepper. Set aside.

CRANBERRY MAPLE GLAZE 1

1 CUP FRESH CRANBERRIES	JUICE OF 1 LEMON
2 CUPS MAPLE SYRUP	1/4 CUP DIJON MUSTARD

Combine all glaze ingredients in a saucepan. Simmer until reduced by one-third. Set aside.

CRANBERRY MAPLE GLAZE 2

1 CUP WHOLE CRANBERRIES	2 CUPS MAPLE SYRUP
IN JELLY	JUICE OF 1 LEMON

Combine all glaze ingredients in a saucepan. Simmer the glaze until reduced by one-third. Use as a glaze or serve as a sauce on the side with the roast chicken breasts.

METHOD OF PREPARATION

Lightly pound the chicken breasts, leaving the skin on. Divide the Old-Fashioned Sage Dressing among the chicken breasts, and stuff. Place in a baking dish and season with salt, pepper, granular garlic, paprika, and chopped parsley. Roast in a 400° F oven for 30–40 minutes or until cooked. Glaze the chickens with the Cranberry Maple Glaze the last 10 minutes of roasting, or serve the sauce on the side.

ROAST BREAST OF CHICKEN
IN A CURRIED CHOPPED
MUSHROOM CREAM SAUCE

SERVES 8

4 ONE-POUND BONE-IN

CHICKEN BREASTS

PAPRIKA TO TASTE

GARLIC POWDER TO TASTE

CHOPPED PARSLEY TO TASTE

CURRIED MUSHROOM CREAM

SAUCE

CURRIED CHOPPED MUSHROOM
CREAM SAUCE

1 STICK UNSALTED BUTTER

2 CUPS CHOPPED MUSHROOMS

1/2 CUP FLOUR

1 CUP WHITE WINE

1 CUP CHICKEN STOCK

1 CHICKEN BOUILLON CUBE

(OPTIONAL)

2 CUPS HEAVY CREAM

1 TABLESPOON CURRY POWDER

Melt the butter in a saucepan, and cook the mushrooms until limp. Add the flour, and stir to make a roux. Add the wine and stock, and stir until smooth. Add the cream and curry powder, and stir until smooth. Simmer the sauce over low heat for 7–10 minutes. Season with salt and pepper. Set aside.

METHOD OF PREPARATION

Rinse the chicken breasts under cold water, and pat dry. Split the chicken breasts in half with a French knife. Place in a roasting pan and season with salt, pepper, granular garlic, paprika, and chopped parsley. Roast in a 400° F oven for 30–40 minutes or until cooked. Pour the Curried Mushroom Cream Sauce over the roasted chicken breasts. Serve.

ROAST BREAST OF CHICKEN WITH
A RED WINE BLUEBERRY GLAZE

SERVES 8

RED WINE BLUEBERRY GLAZE

1 CUP RED WINE

1 CUP MAPLE SYRUP

¼ CUP DIJON MUSTARD

1 PINT FRESH BLUEBERRIES,

PICKED OVER AND

WASHED.

Combine all glaze ingredients in a saucepan. Simmer the sauce until reduced by one-third. Glaze the chickens the last 10 minutes of cooking.

METHOD OF PREPARATION

Follow the Method of Preparation for Roast Breast of Chicken in a Curried Mushroom Cream Sauce, p. 98.

ROAST BREAST OF CHICKEN

IN A PEACH CONSERVE

WHITE WINE WALNUT GLAZE

SERVES 8

PEACH CONSERVE WHITE WINE
WALNUT GLAZE

2 CUPS PEACH CONSERVE	1 TEASPOON FRESHLY GRATED
1 CUP WHITE WINE	GINGER ROOT
1 CUP WALNUT PIECES	

Combine all glaze ingredients in a saucepan. Simmer until reduced by one-third. Glaze the chickens the last 10 minutes of cooking.

METHOD OF PREPARATION

Follow the Method Of Preparation for Roast Breast of Chicken In A Curried Mushroom Cream Sauce, p. 98.

ROAST BREAST OF CHICKEN
IN A PEAR CONSERVE HAZELNUT
WHITE CURRANT GLAZE

SERVES 8

PEAR CONSERVE HAZELNUT
WHITE CURRANT GLAZE

2 RIPE PEARS, CORED AND	1 CUP WHITE CURRANTS
DICED	1 CUP HARD CIDER
1 CUP HAZELNUTS, TOASTED	$1/4$ CUP MAPLE SYRUP
AND CHOPPED	$1/4$ CUP DIJON MUSTARD

Combine all glaze ingredients in a saucepan. Simmer the sauce until reduced by one-third. Glaze the chickens the last 10 minutes of cooking.

METHOD OF PREPARATION

Follow the Method of Preparation for Roast Breast of Chicken in a Curried Mushroom Cream Sauce, p. 98.

ROAST BREAST OF CHICKEN

WITH SHRIMP IN AN

APPLE CIDER CREAM SAUCE

SERVES 8

APPLE CIDER CREAM SAUCE

1 STICK UNSALTED BUTTER	1 CUP CIDER
1/2 CUP FLOUR	1 CUP HEAVY CREAM
2 CUPS CHICKEN STOCK	2 CUPS MAINE SHRIMP, PEELED

Melt the butter in a saucepan. Add the flour, and stir to make a roux. Add the stock and cider, and stir until smooth. Add the heavy cream. Simmer the sauce 7–10 minutes. Add the shrimp, and simmer only until the shrimp are cooked. Season with salt and pepper. Pour the Apple Cider Cream Sauce over the roasted chicken breasts.

METHOD OF PREPARATION

Follow the Method of Preparation for Roast Breast of Chicken in a Curried Mushroom Cream Sauce.

We felt that the simple recipe for chicken potpie, though perfect in its simplicity, was not a luxurious enough dish to command the price asked at dinner at the Creamery, though I must admit that as far as I am concerned the prices were far lower than at comparable establishments. But, in the Shaker tradition of giving people their money's worth, we devised the following recipe based on the ever-favorite chicken potpie.

CHICKEN AND PEAR PIE

SERVES 8

SAUCE

½ STICK UNSALTED BUTTER	2 CUPS CHICKEN STOCK
¼ CUP FLOUR	1 CUP HEAVY CREAM

Melt the half-stick butter in a saucepan. Add the flour, and stir to make a roux. Add the stock and cream, and stir until smooth. Simmer the sauce 7–10 minutes. Season with salt and pepper. Set aside.

METHOD OF PREPARATION

24 PEARS	2 POUNDS COOKED CHICKEN
1 TABLESPOON UNSALTED	MEAT, CUT IN BITE-SIZE
BUTTER	PIECES
¼ CUP HONEY	PASTRY CRUST (OPTIONAL)
1 TABLESPOON LEMON JUICE	

Wash, core, and thinly slice the pears. Sauté the pears in the butter, honey, and lemon juice 3–5 minutes until they start to soften. Remove the pears from the pan, and place in the bottom of a casserole dish or pie dish. Place the cooked chicken meat on top of the cooked pears. Pour the Sauce over the chicken. Top with pastry crust, if desired. Bake in a 400° F oven for 10–15 minutes. Serve.

BEEF

POT ROAST

The Shakers loved pot roast. In Eldress Bertha Lindsay's latest cookbook, *Seasoned with Grace: My Generation of Shaker Cooking,* she writes about Brother Irving Greenwood's Pot Roast. He was not the cook; he was the critic. There is a large old sepia photograph of him from the twenties in one of the rooms where Sister Ethel lives—a handsome man with very disarming eyes that, even from a photograph, make you feel tender toward him. Eldress Bertha jokingly remarks that, though he didn't always compliment the Sisters, he was always very quick to let them know when their cooking wasn't up to par, in particular, the pot roast.

We have included a few variations on the old pot roast. Pot roast seems to be another of those foods that have begun to disappear from tables. Perhaps more and more people are afraid to eat red meat thanks to agribusiness farmers and ranchers who insist upon using chemicals and steroids in the raising of beef. Or perhaps there are fewer large families and more two-person families who think a roast is too much food or too much money. I think that even if you live alone it is wise to "invest" in a pot roast. You can have it the first night as a pot roast, the second night as a stew, and the third in a potpie or sliced cold in a sandwich. Here is a good recipe to get you off the ground.

POT ROAST WITH RED WINE MUSHROOM SAUCE

SERVES 6

3–4 TABLESPOONS OLIVE OIL

3–4 POUND BEEF CHUCK
ROAST

$^1/_2$ CUP FLOUR

1 MEDIUM ONION, CHOPPED

2 TABLESPOONS MINCED
GARLIC

$^1/_2$ POUND SLICED MUSHROOMS

2 TABLESPOONS MINCED HERBS
OF CHOICE

2 CUPS RED WINE

Heat the olive oil in a braising pan on top of the stove. Lightly dust the meat with the flour. Sear the meat in the pan on all sides until browned. Add the onion, garlic, mushrooms, herbs, and the red wine (wine should cover the bottom of the pan half an inch in depth). Cover the pan with foil. Braise in a 350° F oven for 1$^1/_2$–2 hours or until the meat is tender. Slice, and serve with the natural pan drippings.

POT ROAST WITH WHITE
WINE HERB SAUCE

————

SERVES 6

This recipe is an example of the sort of thing you do on a summer evening and serve chilled the next afternoon for lunch, for a cookout, or double the ingredients and serve a crowd.

3–4 TABLESPOONS OLIVE OIL	1 TABLESPOON MINCED SAGE
3–4 POUND BEEF CHUCK	1 TABLESPOON MINCED BASIL
ROAST	1 TABLESPOON MINCED
½ CUP FLOUR	OREGANO
1 MEDIUM ONION, CHOPPED	1 TABLESPOON MINCED THYME
2 TABLESPOONS MINCED	2 CUPS WHITE WINE
GARLIC	

Follow directions for cooking the pot roast in the Pot Roast with Red Wine Mushroom Sauce recipe, p. 105.

CHILLED POT ROAST

WITH A RED WINE MUSHROOM

BLUEBERRY SAUCE

SERVES 6

3–4 TABLESPOONS OLIVE OIL	2 TABLESPOONS MINCED
3–4 POUND BEEF CHUCK	SORREL
ROAST	2 CUPS RED WINE
½ CUP FLOUR	DIJON MUSTARD TO TASTE
1 MEDIUM ONION, CHOPPED	BLUEBERRY CONSERVE TO TASTE
2 CUPS SLICED SHIITAKE	
MUSHROOMS	

Follow directions for cooking the pot roast in the Pot Roast with
Red Wine Mushroom Sauce recipe, p. 105. When the pot roast is
cooked, remove from the pan, cool, and refrigerate overnight.
Pour the cooking liquid into a saucepan, and skim off the grease.
Stir in the mustard and blueberry conserve to taste. Chill the
sauce. Thinly slice the roast, and serve with the chilled sauce.

POT ROAST BRAISED IN SHAKER SWITCHEL WITH WILD MUSHROOMS AND FRESH SAGE

SERVES 6

Switchel was a drink the Shaker Sisters made for the Brothers during haying time when the work was hard and the weather sweltering. They used a barley water in some of the switchel recipes; we've tried to make the recipe a little more accessible. It is a sweet drink, but used in cooking with the fresh sage it is a taste you might never have had before. It gave us great pleasure to come up with this recipe because we felt it was one of the most Shaker-inspired dishes we had conjured up.

3–4 POUND BEEF CHUCK ROAST	1 POUND EDIBLE WILD MUSHROOMS
1 MEDIUM ONION, CHOPPED	1/4 CUP MINCED FRESH SAGE
	2 CUPS SHAKER SWITCHEL

SHAKER SWITCHEL

1/2 CUP BROWN SUGAR	1/3 CUP CIDER VINEGAR
1 QUART WATER	1/2 TEASPOON GRATED
1/4 CUP MOLASSES	GINGER

Combine switchel ingredients in a bowl, stirring until mixed well. Set aside.

METHOD OF PREPARATION

Place the roast in a braising pan, and sear in a 500° F oven for 20 minutes. Add the onion, mushrooms, sage, and switchel to the braising pan. Cover the pan with foil. Braise in a 350° F oven for 1 1/2–2 hours or until the meat is tender. Thinly slice the roast, and serve with the braising sauce.

POT ROAST WITH PEANUT BUTTER

PUMPKIN MUSHROOM SAUCE

SERVES 6

3–4 TABLESPOONS OLIVE OIL	½ CUP FLOUR
3–4 POUND BEEF CHUCK	2 CUPS BEEF STOCK
ROAST	

Heat the olive oil in a braising pan on top of the stove. Lightly dust the roast in the flour. Sear the meat in the pan until browned on all sides. Add the beef stock. Cover the pan with foil. Braise in a 350° F oven for 1½–2 hours or until meat is tender. Reserve braising liquid for sauce.

PEANUT BUTTER PUMPKIN
MUSHROOM SAUCE

2 CUPS PUMPKIN PUREE	1 CUP WHITE WINE
1 CUP BRAISING LIQUID	¼ CUP PEANUT BUTTER
1 BEEF BOUILLON CUBE	2 CUPS SLICED MUSHROOMS
(OPTIONAL)	

Combine the sauce ingredients in a saucepan, and stir until well mixed. Simmer for 10–15 minutes. If the sauce is too thick, thin with a little more braising liquid. Season with salt and pepper. Slice the roast thinly, and serve with the sauce.

BARBECUED BEEF SHORT RIBS

SERVES 8

1/4 CUP OLIVE OIL	POULTRY SEASONING TO TASTE
24 BEEF SHORT RIBS (3 PER PERSON)	GRANULAR GARLIC, TO TASTE
	RED WINE
GROUND ALLSPICE TO TASTE	BARBECUE GLAZE

BARBECUE GLAZE

4 CUPS MAPLE SYRUP	2 MEDIUM ONIONS, CHOPPED
2 CUPS TOMATO SAUCE	2 MEDIUM APPLES, CORED AND CHOPPED
1/2 CUP DIJON MUSTARD	
2 TABLESPOONS GRATED GINGER	4 TEASPOONS CRUSHED RED PEPPER FLAKES

Combine all glaze ingredients in a saucepan. Simmer until reduced by one-third, or to a medium syrup consistency. Set aside.

METHOD OF PREPARATION

On top of the stove heat the olive oil in a braising pan. Add the ribs, and sear on all sides. Season with salt, pepper, ground allspice, poultry seasoning, and granular garlic to taste. When all the ribs have been seared, drain off the grease. Add enough red wine to fill the braising pan half full. Cover the pan with foil. Braise in a 350° F oven for 1 1/2–2 hours or until the ribs are tender. The last 15 minutes of cooking, drain off the braising liquid, add the Barbecue Glaze, and finish cooking uncovered. Season with salt and pepper. Serve.

LAMB

Most of the recipes we found for lamb were more traditional than inventive. Not that there is anything wrong with tradition, but we felt maybe more people who didn't like lamb would try lamb if someone could figure out something else to do with it other than serve it with mint jelly. These are something else!

ROAST LEG OF LAMB WITH
RASPBERRY HORSERADISH SAUCE

SERVES 6–8

4–5 POUND BONELESS LEG	4 BAY LEAVES
OF LAMB ROAST	RASPBERRY HORSERADISH
1 TABLESPOON CRUSHED	SAUCE
GARLIC	

RASPBERRY HORSERADISH SAUCE

2 CUPS RED WINE	1/2 CUP PECAN PIECES
1 CUP RASPBERRY JAM	GRANULATED SUGAR TO TASTE
1/2 MEDIUM ONION, MINCED	GROUND NUTMEG TO TASTE
2 TABLESPOONS HORSERADISH	

Combine sauce ingredients in a saucepan. Simmer until reduced by half. Puree in a blender until smooth. Set aside.

METHOD OF PREPARATION

Season the boneless leg of lamb roast with salt, pepper, crushed garlic, and bay leaves. Roast in a 500° F oven, 20 minutes per pound. Allow the roast to stand 10–15 minutes out of the oven before carving. Serve each portion of sliced lamb with a dollop of the Raspberry Horseradish Sauce, like a condiment.

BRAISED LEG OF MUTTON WITH BROWN SUGAR STUFFING OR PEACH STUFFING IN A NATURAL PAN GRAVY

SERVES 6–8

4–5 POUND BONELESS LEG OF MUTTON OR LAMB ROAST, BUTTERFLIED	BROWN SUGAR STUFFING OR PEACH STUFFING
	RED WINE
	NATURAL PAN GRAVY

BROWN SUGAR STUFFING

4 CUPS TOASTED AND CRUMBLED BREAD	1/2 CUP WHITE WINE
3/4 CUP BROWN SUGAR	1 MEDIUM ONION, MINCED
2 EGGS, BEATEN	2 TABLESPOONS HERBS DE PROVENCE
1 CUP BUTTERMILK	2 TABLESPOONS MINCED SAGE

Combine all stuffing ingredients in a bowl, and mix well by hand until incorporated. Season with salt and pepper. Set aside.

PEACH STUFFING

3 CUPS TOASTED AND	2 EGGS, BEATEN
CRUMBLED BREAD	1 TABLESPOON MINCED GARLIC
2 CUPS PEACH CONSERVE	1 TABLESPOON MINCED SAGE

Combine all stuffing ingredients in a bowl, and mix well by hand until incorporated. Season with salt and pepper. Set aside.

METHOD OF PREPARATION

Ask your butcher to butterfly the boneless leg of mutton or lamb roast. Stuff the roast with the stuffing of your choice, and tie with butcher's twine to hold the stuffing in. Place in a roasting pan, and season with salt and pepper. Add red wine to a depth of half an inch in the bottom of the roasting pan. Cover the pan with foil. Braise in a 500° F oven for 1–1½ hours. Reserve pan drippings for gravy.

NATURAL PAN GRAVY

3 CUPS PAN DRIPPINGS	2–3 TABLESPOONS FLOUR

Pour the pan drippings into a blender with the flour. Mix until the sauce becomes smooth. Simmer the sauce in a saucepan 5–7 minutes until it thickens. Season with salt and pepper. Thinly slice the roast, and serve with the Pan Gravy.

PORK

_____

For a short time in the 1830s there was a movement among the Shakers to abstain not only from meat but specifically from all pork products. Part of the reason had to do with the belief that pork made people more accessible to carnal temptations. Another reason for this abstention stems from the old biblical claims that pork meat was unclean. But even from the founding of the first Shaker "families" in the late 1700s there is evidence that pork was one of their most widely enjoyed victuals. It was from popular demand that meat, and especially pork products, were finally returned to the Shaker tables.

ROAST LOIN OF PORK WITH

SHAKER-STYLE VENISON SAUCE

_____

SERVES 6–8

4–5 POUND BONELESS PORK LOIN ROAST	RED WINE SHAKER-STYLE VENISON SAUCE

SHAKER-STYLE
VENISON SAUCE

1 CUP PAN DRIPPINGS, GREASE REMOVED	BLACKBERRY BRANDY*
	1 CUP BLACK CURRANT JELLY*
1 CUP BROWN SUGAR	1/4 CUP DIJON MUSTARD

Combine sauce ingredients in a saucepan. Simmer 5–10 minutes. Set aside.

*You may substitute any combination of liquer and jelly.

METHOD OF PREPARATION

Place the pork roast in a roasting pan, and season with salt and pepper. Sear in a 450° F oven for 20–30 minutes. Add red wine to depth of half an inch in the bottom of the roasting pan. Cover the pan with foil. Cook in a 400° F oven, 30 minutes to the pound. Reserve pan drippings for the sauce. Thinly slice the roast, and serve with the Shaker-Style Venison Sauce.

ROAST LOIN OF PORK WITH AN APPLE, SAUSAGE, AND GREEN ONION STUFFING IN A DARK SAGE GRAVY

SERVES 6–8

4–5 POUND BONELESS PORK LOIN, BUTTERFLIED	1/4 CUP CHOPPED FRESH SAGE
APPLE, SAUSAGE, AND GREEN ONION STUFFING	RED WINE
	DARK SAGE GRAVY

APPLE, SAUSAGE, AND GREEN ONION STUFFING

3/4 CUP CUBED BREAD	1 EGG YOLK
4 TABLESPOONS MILK	1/2 CUP CHOPPED GREEN ONIONS
1 POUND PORK SAUSAGE MEAT	2 TABLESPOONS MINCED GARLIC
1 1/4 CUPS DRIED APPLES	
2 EGGS, BEATEN	

Soak the bread in the milk 10 minutes. in a mixing bowl combine all of the stuffing ingredients, and mix well by hand. Season with salt and pepper. Set aside.

METHOD OF PREPARATION

Spread the Apple, Sausage, and Green Onion Stuffing evenly over the butterflied pork loin, and roll up. Tie with butcher's twine to hold the stuffing in, and place in a roasting pan. Sear in a 500° F oven for 20–30 minutes. Sprinkle on the sage, and add the red wine to a depth of half an inch in the bottom of the roasting pan. Cover the pan with foil. Cook in a 400° F oven, 30 minutes per pound. Reserve pan drippings for gravy.

DARK SAGE GRAVY

PAN DRIPPINGS | 1–2 TABLESPOONS FLOUR

Pour the pan drippings and flour into a blender. Mix until smooth. Simmer in a saucepan 7–10 minutes until thickened. Season with salt and pepper. Thinly slice the roast, and serve with the Dark Sage Gravy.

ROAST LOIN OF PORK WITH

AN APPLE SAUSAGE SAGE STUFFING

WITH RED WINE GRAVY

SERVES 4–6

APPLE SAUSAGE SAGE STUFFING

2 CUPS PORK SAUSAGE MEAT	2 EGGS, BEATEN
1 CUP DICED APPLES	1/2 CUP RED WINE
3/4 CUP CHOPPED SCALLIONS	1 TABLESPOON MINCED SAGE

Combine all stuffing ingredients in a food processor, and chop coarsely. Season with salt and pepper. Set aside.

METHOD OF PREPARATION

Follow directions for Roast Loin of Pork with an Apple, Sausage, and Green Onion Stuffing in a Dark Sage Gravy, p. 118.

BONELESS PORK STEAKS
BAKED IN AN APPLE AND
ONION CIDER CREAM SAUCE

SERVES 8

1/4 CUP OLIVE OIL

16 THREE-TO-FOUR-OUNCE

BONELESS PORK STEAKS

GRANULAR GARLIC TO TASTE

GROUND GINGER TO TASTE

1/2 TEASPOON BROWN SUGAR

PER STEAK

APPLE AND ONION CIDER CREAM SAUCE

3 MEDIUM APPLES, SLICED

1 MEDIUM ONION, SLICED

2 CUPS CIDER OR APPLE JUICE

CONCENTRATE

3 CUPS HEAVY CREAM

Combine all ingredients in a saucepan and reduce by one-third. Set aside.

METHOD OF PREPARATION

Heat the olive oil in a skillet, and brown the pork steaks on both sides. Season the steaks with salt, pepper, granular garlic, ground ginger, and brown sugar. Place in a baking dish. Cook in a 400° F oven for 30 minutes. Remove the pork from oven, and drain off the grease. Pour the Apple and Onion Cider Cream Sauce over the steaks, and return them to the oven for another 20–30 minutes. Season with salt and pepper. Serve.

ROAST LOIN OF PORK WITH
A WHITE WINE PUMPKIN SAUCE

SERVES 6–8

4–5 POUND BONELESS PORK LOIN ROAST	2 CUPS WHITE WINE
	WHITE WINE PUMPKIN SAUCE

METHOD OF PREPARATION

Season the pork roast with salt and pepper. Place in a roasting pan, and sear in a 450° F oven for 20–30 minutes. Add white wine to a depth of half an inch in the bottom of the roasting pan. Cover pan with foil. Cook in a 400° F oven, 30 minutes per pound. Reserve the braising liquid for the sauce.

WHITE WINE PUMPKIN SAUCE

1/2 STICK UNSALTED BUTTER	1 CUP PUMPKIN PUREE
1 TEASPOON MINCED GARLIC	BRAISING LIQUID
1/2 CUP SLICED LEEKS	1 BEEF BOUILLON CUBE
1/4 CUP FLOUR	(OPTIONAL)
1 CUP WHITE WINE	

Melt the butter in a saucepan, and cook the garlic and leeks until limp. Stir in the flour to make a roux. Add the white wine and stir until smooth. Add the pumpkin puree, and stir until smooth. Simmer on very low heat 10–15 minutes. Thin with the braising liquid as necessary. Season with salt and pepper. Thinly slice the pork roast and serve with the White Wine Pumpkin Sauce.

ROAST PORK WITH SAUERKRAUT, MUSHROOMS, AND CIDER

SERVES 8

4–5 POUND BONELESS PORK LOIN ROAST	2 CUPS APPLE CIDER
	2 CUPS SLICED MUSHROOMS
1/2 CUP FLOUR	2 CUPS DICED ONIONS
1/4 CUP OLIVE OIL	1 CUP SAUERKRAUT
2 CUPS RED WINE	

METHOD OF PREPARATION

Season the pork loin with salt and pepper. Lightly dust the roast with flour. On the top of the stove, heat the olive oil in a braising pan, and sear the roast until browned on all sides. Drain off all of the grease. Add the wine, cider, mushrooms, onions, and sauerkraut. Cover the pan with foil. Cook in a 400° F oven for 1 1/2–2 hours. Thinly slice the roast, and serve with the pan drippings.

ROAST LOIN OF PORK
WITH APPLE SAGE DRESSING
IN A CRANBERRY SAUCE

SERVES 8

4–5 POUND BONELESS PORK	WHITE WINE
LOIN, BUTTERFLIED	CRANBERRY SAUCE
APPLE SAGE DRESSING	

APPLE SAGE DRESSING

2 CUPS CHOPPED DRIED APPLES	2 TABLESPOONS CHOPPED
1 CUP DICED ONIONS	PARSLEY
2 CUPS BREAD CRUMBS	2 TABLESPOONS MINCED SAGE
1 CUP WINE OR BUTTERMILK	1 TABLESPOON MINCED GARLIC
3 EGGS, BEATEN	1 STICK UNSALTED BUTTER,
	MELTED

Combine all dressing ingredients in a bowl, and mix well by hand. Season with salt and pepper. Set aside.

METHOD OF PREPARATION

Evenly spread the Apple Sage Dressing over the butterflied pork roast, and roll it up. Tie with butcher's twine to hold the stuffing in. Sear in a 450° F oven for 20–30 minutes. Drain off the grease. Add white wine to a depth of half an inch in the bottom of the roasting pan. Cover the pan with foil. Cook in a 400° F oven for 1¹/₂–2 hours. Reserve the braising liquid for the sauce.

CRANBERRY SAUCE

12-OUNCE BAG FRESH	1 CUP GRANULATED SUGAR
CRANBERRIES	2 CUPS BRAISING LIQUID
1 CUP RED WINE	

Combine sauce ingredients in a saucepan. Simmer until the cranberries burst. Season with salt and pepper. Thinly slice the roast, and serve with the Cranberry Sauce.

HAM

BAKED HAM WITH AN
APPLE CIDER GLAZE

SERVES 6–8

APPLE CIDER GLAZE

1 CUP APPLE JUICE CONCENTRATE	½ CUP DIJON MUSTARD
1 CUP MAPLE SYRUP	2 ORANGES, SEEDED AND SLICED

Combine the glaze ingredients in a saucepan. Simmer the sauce until reduced by half. Pour the glaze over your favorite baked ham recipe during the last 15 minutes of cooking, or pour over grilled ham steaks. Serve.

BAKED HAM WITH
A BLACKBERRY RASPBERRY
RED WINE SAUCE

SERVES 6–8

BLACKBERRY RASPBERRY
RED WINE SAUCE

2 CUPS RED WINE	1/2 PINT FRESH BLACKBERRIES
1 CUP BROWN SUGAR	1/2 PINT FRESH RASPBERRIES
2 TABLESPOONS DIJON	
MUSTARD	

Combine the wine and brown sugar in a saucepan, and heat until reduced by half. Stir in the mustard, blackberries, and raspberries. Serve over your favorite baked ham recipe or over grilled ham steaks.

FOUR

VEGETABLES

The Shakers always planted extra rows of vegetables. Some went to the crows, the rest went to the thieves. We do the same thing today, only instead of crows and thieves we do it for the politicians and the IRS.

For those of us who are fortunate enough to have a patch of land on which to grow fresh herbs and vegetables, the result goes well beyond the effort. Even in the cities, if you can only have a flower box or a couple of pots on a window ledge or fire escape, you ought to try growing something simple, maybe a little fresh basil or oregano, maybe a tomato or pepper plant. I have no idea how it might affect the economy if the millions of people living in cities grew tomato plants in window boxes, but I do know their sense of accomplishment would give them a feeling of satisfaction rarely found anywhere.

It was nothing short of luxury for the Shakers to be able to pick something from their gardens and within the hour be cooking and eating it. It was a luxury of taste and freshness, and that greatest of all luxuries, the healthiest product they could put into their bodies—three commodities that seem to be going the way of the lobster and the chicken wing. The following recipes should be considered necessities.

CHILLED ASPARAGUS IN

A CUMIN VINAIGRETTE

SERVES 8

2 POUNDS FRESH ASPARAGUS

WATER TO COVER

$^2/_3$ CUP OLIVE OIL

$^1/_3$ CUP RED WINE VINEGAR

1–2 TABLESPOONS CUMIN

Poach the asparagus in salted water until tender. Chill. Combine the oil, vinegar, and cumin in a blender, and mix for 30 seconds. Pour the dressing over the chilled asparagus, season with salt and pepper, and serve.

CHILLED CURRIED

ASPARAGUS

SERVES 8

2 POUNDS FRESH ASPARAGUS

WATER TO COVER

1½ CUPS OLIVE OIL

⅓ CUP RED WINE VINEGAR

½ CUP FRESH LIME JUICE

1 TABLESPOON MINCED GARLIC

1 TABLESPOON CURRY POWDER

Poach the asparagus in salted water until tender. Chill. Combine the oil, vinegar, lime juice, garlic, and curry powder in a blender, and mix for 30 seconds. Pour the dressing over the chilled asparagus, season with salt and pepper, and serve.

STEAMED ASPARAGUS IN

A LEMON CORIANDER BUTTER

SERVES 8

1 STICK PLUS 5 TABLESPOONS	⅓ CUP FRESH LEMON JUICE
UNSALTED BUTTER	2 POUNDS FRESH ASPARAGUS
1 TABLESPOON GROUND	
CORIANDER	

In a saucepan heat the butter, coriander, and lemon juice until hot. Steam the asparagus until tender. Pour the flavored butter over the hot asparagus. Season with salt and pepper. Serve.

GREEN BEANS BAKED IN

AN HERBED OLIVE OIL

SERVES 8

2 POUNDS FRESH GREEN BEANS	2 TABLESPOONS MINCED FRESH
1/4 CUP OLIVE OIL	HERBS OF CHOICE

Wash the green beans and trim the ends. Combine oil with herbs and toss well with the beans. Place in a baking dish, cover with foil, and bake in a 400° F oven for 30 minutes or until tender. Season with salt and pepper. Serve hot.

GINGERED BEETS

SERVES 8

2 POUNDS BEETS, WASHED
AND SLICED

1 CUP APPLE JUICE
CONCENTRATE

1/2–3/4 CUP HONEY OR
MAPLE SYRUP

1 1/2 TABLESPOONS MINCED
GINGER

2 TABLESPOONS CORNSTARCH

1/2 CUP CIDER VINEGAR

Place the sliced beets in a baking dish. Combine the apple juice
concentrate, honey or maple syrup, ginger, cornstarch, and
vinegar in a blender, and mix for 30 seconds. Pour the sauce
over the beets, cover with foil, and bake in a 400° F over for
30 minutes or until tender. Serve.

BROCCOLI SAUTÉED IN A
RED PEPPER FENNEL BUTTER

SERVES 4–6

1 LARGE HEAD OF BROCCOLI	1 STICK UNSALTED BUTTER
1 MEDIUM RED BELL PEPPER	$^1/_4$ CUP CHOPPED FENNEL

Wash the broccoli and trim into florets. Peel and slice the stalk. Wash, seed, and thinly slice the pepper. In a skillet melt the butter. Add the red pepper, fennel, and broccoli, and sauté over medium heat until the broccoli is tender. Season with salt and pepper. Serve.

STEAMED BROCCOLI WITH

SESAME CUMIN BUTTER

SERVES 4–6

1 LARGE HEAD OF BROCCOLI	1 TABLESPOON TOASTED
1 STICK UNSALTED BUTTER	SESAME SEEDS
1 TABLESPOON CUMIN	JUICE OF 1 LEMON

Wash the head of broccoli and remove the stem. Place the head of broccoli in a steamer, and cook until tender. In a saucepan melt the butter with the cumin, sesame seeds, and lemon juice until hot. Pour the hot butter over the hot head of broccoli. Season with salt and pepper. Serve.

BROCCOLI BAKED IN A GINGER APPLE BUTTER WITH ROSE PEPPERCORNS

SERVES 4–6

1 LARGE HEAD OF BROCCOLI

1 CUP APPLE BUTTER

¼ CUP CHICKEN STOCK

1 TABLESPOON MINCED GINGER

1 TABLESPOON ROSE PEPPERCORNS

1 TABLESPOON OLIVE OIL

Wash the broccoli and trim into florets. Steam for 5–7 minutes, then cool. Place the parcooked broccoli in a baking dish. Combine the apple butter, stock, ginger, peppercorns, and olive oil, and mix until incorporated. Pour the sauce over the broccoli. Cover with foil, and bake in a 400° F oven for 30 minutes. Season with salt and pepper. Serve.

BRUSSELS SPROUTS SAUTÉED IN

A SPEARMINT OLIVE OIL

SERVES 4

1 POUND BRUSSELS SPROUTS	2 TABLESPOONS CHOPPED
1/4 CUP OLIVE OIL	FRESH SPEARMINT

Wash and trim the Brussels sprouts. In a frying pan heat the oil. Add the Brussels sprouts and spearmint. Cook over medium heat for 10 minutes or until the Brussels sprouts are tender. Season with salt and pepper. Serve.

BRUSSELS SPROUTS AND

PEARL ONIONS

FLAMBÉED IN COGNAC

SERVES 4

1 POUND BRUSSELS SPROUTS	$^1/_4$ CUP OLIVE OIL
$^1/_2$ POUND PEARL ONIONS	$^1/_4$ CUP COGNAC

Wash and trim the Brussels sprouts and pearl onions. Heat the oil in a frying pan. Add the Brussels sprouts and onions, and cook over medium heat for 5–7 minutes. Add the cognac and flambé. Continue to cook another 5 minutes or until tender. Season with salt and pepper. Serve.

BUTTERNUT SQUASH

Most winter squashes need to be peeled and cooked, and then cooked one more time into the recipe you intend making. Here's a little cooking lesson about winter squashes and pumpkins.

PURÉE OF BUTTERNUT SQUASH WITH CRANBERRIES AND BROWN SUGAR

SERVES 4–6

1 MEDIUM (1½-POUND) BUTTERNUT SQUASH, PUMPKIN, OR BANANA SQUASH	1 CUP FRESH CRANBERRIES
	2 CUPS LIGHT BROWN SUGAR
	NUTMEG TO TASTE
	2 CUPS APPLE CIDER

Take a medium-sized butternut squash, or pumpkin or banana squash. Cut it in half, scrape out the seeds, peel it, and cut it into 2-inch-sized cubes. Put the squash into a saucepan with 1 cup of fresh cranberries, 2 cups of light brown sugar, 2 cups of apple cider. Season with a little salt and pepper and maybe a teaspoon or more of nutmeg. Very simple. Bring the mixture to a boil, and immediately turn low to a simmer, stirring every 10–15 minutes to keep the mixture from sticking to the bottom of the pan. Let it cook on a low heat for about 30–45 minutes or however long it takes until the berries have burst and the squash is soft to the touch. Take it off the stove and mash the mixture like mashed potatoes. Put it all into a buttered baking dish, sprinkle with brown sugar and butter, and bake in a 400° F oven for 15–20 minutes.

What you've just learned is "how to do it." What you do it with is entirely up to your personal taste. Try parsnips and cranberries, carrots and cranberries, or beets and cranberries. Finding new ways to "Shaker your plate."

GREEN CABBAGE SAUTÉED

IN CUMIN BUTTER

————

SERVES 4–6

| 1 SMALL HEAD OF GREEN | 1 STICK UNSALTED BUTTER |
| CABBAGE | 1 TABLESPOON CUMIN |

Wash, core, and thinly slice the cabbage. Melt the butter in a frying pan. Add the cabbage, and cook until the cabbage becomes limp but still hasn't lost its color. Add the cumin, and season with salt and pepper. Serve.

This dish may be served cold as a slaw by substituting 1/2 cup olive oil for the butter.

BAKED CARROTS IN

A MINTED ORANGE GLAZE

SERVES 6–8

2 POUNDS CARROTS	$1/2$ CUP FRESH SPEARMINT
1 CUP ORANGE JUICE	JUICE OF 1 LEMON
CONCENTRATE	$1/4$ CUP UNSALTED BUTTER,
$1/4$ CUP HONEY	MELTED

Wash and scrub the carrots. Cut off the tops and slice thinly.
Place the sliced carrots in a baking dish. Combine in a blender
the orange juice concentrate, honey, spearmint, lemon juice,
and melted butter, and mix for 30 seconds. Pour the sauce over
the carrots, cover with foil, and bake in a 400° F oven for 30
minutes or until tender.

BAKED CARROTS IN

NEW HAMPSHIRE MAPLE SYRUP

SERVES 6–8

2 POUNDS CARROTS	1 STICK UNSALTED BUTTER,
1 CUP NEW HAMPSHIRE	MELTED
MAPLE SYRUP	

Scrub, but don't peel, the carrots. Cut off their hats and tails. If you prefer, the carrots can be diced or sliced; I prefer to cook them whole. Place the carrots in a baking dish. Pour maple syrup and melted butter over the top. Season with salt and pepper. Cover tightly and bake in a 400° F oven for 30 minutes or until carrots soften. Uncover the carrots and bake another 10–15 minutes.

CAULIFLOWER

―――――

This is one of those vegetables that most kids hate. It looks dumb to a kid, and the name can be confusing. When I was a little kid, I thought it was a flower you brought to collies that would make them happy, kind of like the flowers you lay on a May altar. And then the collie would smile benignly at you and give you some kind of a dog blessing. Collies were the only dogs I wasn't terrified of, so I suppose in some sense I got what I expected. Surprisingly, I also liked the vegetable.

There is talk that the cauliflower is a wonder vegetable that, if eaten regularly, can help to avoid the risk of cancer. I would like to think the possibility exists. I suppose if you told this to kids they wouldn't eat cauliflower until they were past fifty. The following recipes do some nice things with cauliflower. You could eat the first dish hot or chilled.

CAULIFLOWER IN AN HERBAL

SOUR CREAM SAUCE

SERVES 4–6

1 LARGE HEAD OF
CAULIFLOWER

2 TABLESPOONS UNSALTED
BUTTER

1 TABLESPOON MINCED GARLIC

2 TABLESPOONS FLOUR

1/2 CUP WHITE WINE OR MADEIRA

2 CUPS SOUR CREAM

2 TABLESPOONS MINCED FRESH
HERBS OF CHOICE

Wash and cut the cauliflower into florets. Set aside. In a
saucepan melt the butter, and sauté the garlic 1 minute. Add the
flour, and stir to make a roux. Stir in the wine or Madeira until
smooth. Stir in the sour cream and minced herbs. Simmer over
low heat for 10–15 minutes. Steam the cauliflower until tender.
Pour the sauce over the cauliflower. Season with salt and pepper.
Serve.

BAKED CAULIFLOWER
TOPPED WITH A CURRIED
ROASTED ONION SAUCE

SERVES 4–6

1 LARGE HEAD OF	2 TABLESPOONS OLIVE OIL
CAULIFLOWER	2 TABLESPOONS CURRY
1 MEDIUM ONION	POWDER

Wash and trim the bottom of the cauliflower, leaving whole. Peel and thinly slice the onion. Place the head of cauliflower and the sliced onion in a buttered baking dish. Mix the oil and curry powder until incorporated, and pour over the vegetables. Cover with foil, and bake in a 400° F oven for 30 minutes or until the cauliflower is tender. Season with salt and pepper. Serve.

CORN

_____

Nothing is more American than corn. Even its colors, green and yellow, signify growth and energy. The North American Indians saved the lives of the early colonists by teaching them how to plant corn. Most of the early colonists—people who came to this country to escape persecution—repayed the Indians by stealing their land, decimating their families and tribes, destroying their traditions, enslaving as many of them as they could, and breaking every single pact ever made. Perhaps all anyone learns from oppression is how to persecute. The Shakers recognized the Indians as human beings partly because they shared the same kind of oppression and partly because of their understanding of Christianity and equality. Ah, two more going the way of the chicken wing and lobster.

Corn! Freshly picked, husked as you bring it in from the garden, and cooked within three minutes of picking. A little salt, a lot of butter, and plenty of napkins. An original fast food. My grandmother in Indiana used to call corn "roastin' ears." That's because some people used to toss entire cobs, husks and silks and all, into a fire and take them out when they steamed. You can take corn off the cob, cream it, make it into a pudding, turn it into a chowder, or bake it whole in maple syrup or honey. Or you could grind the kernels into flour, then make cornbread and fritters, corn cakes, cornflakes, and, of course, Indian pudding.

SHAKER-STYLE

CORN PUDDING

————

SERVES 4

This dish is not a dessert but a vegetable. With just a little imagination
(and a lot more sugar) it could be a very interesting baked pudding, not
unlike rice pudding.

2 EGGS	2 CUPS CORN
1 EGG YOLK	1 CUP BREAD CRUMBS
1 TABLESPOON BROWN SUGAR	2 TABLESPOONS UNSALTED
1 CUP HEAVY CREAM	BUTTER, MELTED
1/2 CUP SLICED SCALLIONS	

Beat the eggs and sugar until smooth. Mix the egg mixture,
cream, scallions, and corn together. Season with salt and pepper.
Pour into a bake-and-serve dish. Mix the bread crumbs with the
melted butter. Top the corn mixture with buttered bread crumbs.
Bake in a 325° F oven for 45 minutes or until custard is set. Serve.

The trouble with corn is that there has been so much of it, and cooks have done so much to it and with it, that we have begun to lose the forest for the trees, or in this case the cob for the kernels. Corn is terrifically healthful. It is filled with vitamin A, and it tastes great! But how do you get to try something new with corn? You simply experiment, as you would with anything else whether it is untested or has been around for a hundred years. You always have to be seeking out new possibilities.

You can pick little tiny baby ears of corn and pickle them, sauté them in butter, or flambé them in brandy or Amaretto. You can bread them and fry them in olive oil with garlic and lemon. There are almost endless possibilities using baby corn.

As for old corn, other than my own, I don't recall ever having used any other than popping corn. In the very early days of this country people often boiled dried corn in water and bear grease. The result was probably filled with protein and vitamins A and B, and it might even have been tasty. Sometimes maple syrup, honey, or fresh fruit would be added, or milk poured over it.

What a wonderful thing a stalk of corn is! With all that it possesses in terms of the power to sustain life, it is not surprising that corn is the symbol of fertility of the earth, the awakening of life.

I'm not so certain I want to trust the growing of anything as important as the vegetables I eat to agribusiness here or abroad. There might be lower prices in the market and foods out of season, but there is a trade-off. You are also buying fruits and vegetables that have been sprayed, dyed, picked before their time, and shipped thousands of miles. By the time a vegetable gets to your table it has very little taste, less nutritional value, and perhaps even some harmful agents thanks to the spraying, dyeing, and fertilizing—just something you might consider the next time you're picking up a dozen ears of corn in January in Jamestown, North Dakota.

I often wonder how the Shakers would have reacted to agribusiness. And if the current laws governing farming and dairy and meat production would even allow them to exist today. For instance, if Eldress Bertha decided she wanted to sell a few pies and cakes and some bread from her own house, she would find that, according to law, she would have to install another kitchen completely separate from the one that already existed, with five stainless steel sinks and a private bathroom with yet another sink. She would have to take out a mortgage, spend a hundred thousand dollars, and hope that she could sell fifteen hundred dollars' worth of pies and cakes in a month just to pay the bills.

On the other hand, if you are a large bakery, nationally or regionally known, using inferior and less imaginative products to produce a sugary, ersatz cream confection that has a shelf life of a year, you have the money to conform to all the strictures and therefore the right to market a second-rate product. What's really frightening is that quality is never the issue here, only the ability to buy equipment mandated by people who are not cooks. The United States will never have a national cuisine more exciting than the kind of food the government regulates for sale. Well, this is beginning to sound like some of that old corn I mentioned a while back.

CORN ON THE COB

SAUTÉED IN OLIVE OIL

AND FRESH HERBS

SERVES 4–6

4 EARS OF CORN	15 FRESH BASIL LEAVES
½ CUP OLIVE OIL	4–6 SCALLIONS, CUT INTO
1 TABLESPOON MINCED GARLIC	1-INCH PIECES

Husk the corn, and cut the cobs into pieces 1½ inches in length. Heat the oil in a frying pan. Add the corn pieces, garlic, basil, and scallions, and sauté over medium heat until the corn is tender. Season with salt and pepper. Serve.

This is also a great appetizer.

SCALLOPED CORN

SERVES 4–6

½ STICK UNSALTED BUTTER	3 CUPS CORN KERNELS, FRESH
¼ CUP DICED ONION	OR FROZEN
1 CUP DICED RED BELL PEPPER	1 CUP BREAD CRUMBS
¼ CUP FLOUR	2 TABLESPOONS UNSALTED
2½ CUPS MILK	BUTTER, MELTED
1 TABLESPOON DIJON MUSTARD	

Melt the butter in a frying pan. Sauté the onion and red pepper in the butter until soft. Stir in the flour to make a roux. Slowly stir in the milk until smooth. Stir in the mustard. Bring to a simmer and cook 5 minutes. Add the corn. Pour the mixture into a buttered baking dish. Mix the bread crumbs with the melted butter. Top corn mixture with buttered bread crumbs. Bake in a 375° F oven until the bread crumbs are toasted.

POTATOES

————

Potatoes are something I feel one should eat a lot of during the winter months. I have no scientific backup for this statement; it's just something that I feel. There is, however, a kind of security in a baked potato, something whole and familial. Potato soup on chilly damp days, creamed potatoes, when they're new, with fresh scallions, roasted potatoes with olive oil and herbs, mashed potatoes and cream gravy made from the drippings of fried chicken—the kind of food that reminds you of home. At this point of history it is trendy to refer to this kind of cooking as "comfort food." Please don't ever call it that.

CREAMED POTATOES

————

SERVES 4

1 POUND POTATOES	1/2–3/4 CUP WHITE WINE
1/2 CUP OLIVE OIL	1 TABLESPOON MINCED GARLIC
1 TABLESPOON CHICKEN BASE	1 CUP HEAVY CREAM

Wash, peel, and cube the potatoes. Place the potatoes in a baking dish. Combine in a blender the oil, chicken base, wine, and garlic, and mix for 15 seconds. Pour over the potatoes, cover with foil, and bake in a 400° F oven 45–60 minutes. Add the cream, and toss well. Return uncovered to the oven, and allow the potatoes to brown for 10–15 minutes. Season with salt and pepper. Serve.

ROASTED RED POTATOES

IN THEIR JACKETS

WITH HERBS AND RED WINE

SERVES 4–6

2 POUNDS RED POTATOES	2 TABLESPOONS MINCED GARLIC
1/2 CUP OLIVE OIL	3 TABLESPOONS MINCED FRESH
1 CUP RED WINE	HERBS OF CHOICE

Wash and quarter the potatoes. Toss with the remaining ingredients. Place in a baking dish, cover with foil, and bake in a 400° F oven for 45 minutes. Remove the foil, and continue to bake for 15 minutes. Season with salt and pepper. Serve.

BAKED POTATOES STUFFED

WITH CREAMED SPINACH

AND CHEDDAR CHEESE

SERVES 6

3 LARGE BAKING POTATOES	1 POUND SPINACH, PICKED
1 STICK UNSALTED BUTTER,	OVER AND WASHED
MELTED	3/4 CUP HEAVY CREAM
	1 CUP GRATED CHEDDAR CHEESE

Wash the potatoes and bake 45 minutes in a 500° F oven. Combine the melted butter, spinach, cream, and cheese in a food processor, and mix 15 seconds until blended. Slice the potatoes in half lengthwise and remove the pulp. Mash the potato pulp with the cream mixture until blended. Season with salt and pepper. Using a spoon, fill the potato shells with the seasoned potato mixture. Place the stuffed potatoes in a baking pan, and bake in a 500° F oven for 15 minutes. Serve.

SLICED POTATOES BAKED

WITH ONIONS IN PORK STOCK

SERVES 4–6

These potatoes need to be prepared when you're cooking a whole pork roast. It's a very old way of doing potatoes, simple and done in almost every ethnic cuisine that uses potatoes.

4 MEDIUM POTATOES	1 TABLESPOON MINCED SAGE
1 MEDIUM ONION	2 CUPS PORK STOCK

Wash and thinly slice the potatoes. Peel and thinly slice the onion. Lay the potatoes in a baking dish and cover with sliced onions. Sprinkle the minced sage over the potatoes and onions. Add the pork stock. Bake uncovered in a 375° F oven for about 1 hour. Stir often and remember not to thicken the pork stock, which will naturally thicken from the potatoes' starch as they cook.

PARSNIPS BAKED IN

NEW HAMPSHIRE MAPLE SYRUP

SERVES 6–8

8–12 MEDIUM (2 POUNDS)	2 TABLESPOONS BUTTER,
PARSNIPS	MELTED
3/4–1 CUP MAPLE SYRUP	2 TABLESPOONS CINNAMON
	OR CURRY POWDER

The best time to dig parsnips is in the spring after they've sat in the ground for the whole winter. They are a light cream color, the color of the beginning of knowledge, and are sweet with nutrients and vitamins. Scrub, but don't peel, about 8 to 12 medium-sized parsnips. Cut off their hats and tails, cut them into 2-inch cubes, and put into a buttered baking dish. Pour about a cup of maple syrup over the top, add a couple of tablespoons of melted butter, salt and pepper to taste, and add a few sprinkles of cinnamon or curry. Cover tightly and bake at 400° F for 30 minutes, long enough for the parsnips to soften, then uncover and bake another 10–15 minutes.

MAPLE SWEET-POTATO

SOUFFLÉ

SERVES 4–6

4 MEDIUM SWEET POTATOES	2 TEASPOONS GROUND
1/2 CUP MAPLE SYRUP	ALLSPICE
	6 EGG WHITES

Wash and pierce the potatoes and bake in a 500° F oven for 45 minutes. Peel the potatoes, and puree the pulp in a food processor with the maple syrup and allspice until smooth. In a separate bowl, whip the egg whites until medium-stiff peaks form. Gently fold the whipped egg whites into the potato puree. Pour the mixture into a baking dish. Bake in a 400° F oven for 30 minutes. Serve.

TOMATOES BAKED WITH

A LEMON BASIL OIL

SERVES 6

6 MEDIUM TOMATOES	2 CUPS MINCED FRESH BASIL
1 CUP OLIVE OIL	2 TABLESPOONS MINCED GARLIC
1/4 CUP LEMON JUICE	

Slice the tops off the tomatoes, and place in a buttered baking dish. Combine in a blender the oil, lemon juice, basil, and garlic, and mix about 30 seconds until smooth. Pour mixture over the tomatoes. Bake in a 400° F oven for 30 minutes or until the tomatoes are soft. Season with salt and pepper. Serve.

BAKED TOMATO CUSTARD

SERVES 6

This custard can be baked either in a pie crust or in a baking dish.

2 LARGE TOMATOES	1 TABLESPOON GRANULATED
PREPARED PIE SHELL (OPTIONAL)	SUGAR
4 EGGS	2 TABLESPOONS MINCED BASIL
2 EGG YOLKS	1/2 TEASPOON NUTMEG
1 CUP LIGHT CREAM	

Wash and slice the tomatoes. Place them in the pie shell or a buttered baking dish. Combine the eggs, egg yolks, cream, sugar, basil, and nutmeg in a blender, and mix for 15–20 seconds. Pour the mixture over the tomatoes. Bake in a 425° F oven for 10 minutes. Reduce the oven temperature to 300° F, and cook 30 minutes or until the custard is set (when a toothpick is inserted, it comes out clean). Serve hot or cold.

CHILLED MIXED VEGETABLES

IN A LEMON BASIL OIL

SERVES 6–8

6 CUPS CHILLED

    VEGETABLES:

    BROCCOLI FLORETS

    CAULIFLOWER FLORETS

    SLICED CARROTS

1½ CUPS OLIVE OIL

2 CUPS FRESH BASIL

JUICE OF 2 LEMONS

Combine the oil, basil, and lemon juice in a blender, and mix for 30 seconds. Pour the dressing over the chilled cooked vegetables, and marinate in the refrigerator for 4 hours. Season with salt and pepper. Serve.

MIXED VEGETABLE
RICOTTA CUSTARD

———

SERVES 4–6

2 CUPS DICED MIXED VEGETABLES

2 TABLESPOONS BUTTER

2 CUPS RICOTTA CHEESE

2 EGGS

1 TABLESPOON MINCED GARLIC

2 TABLESPOONS MINCED FRESH
OREGANO

1 CUP GRATED MUENSTER CHEESE

Sauté the mixed vegetables in butter (even leftovers work terrifically). In a bowl mix the ricotta, eggs, garlic, and oregano until smooth. Add the cooked mixed vegetables, and mix well. Pour into a baking dish. Top with the grated Muenster cheese. Bake in a 425° F oven for 10 minutes. Reduce the oven temperature to 300° F, and continue to bake for 45 minutes or until the custard becomes thick and the vegetables are tender. Serve.

ZUCCHINI . . . LOOK OUT!

HERE IT COMES AGAIN!

SERVES 4–6

1 MEDIUM ZUCCHINI

1 MEDIUM CANTALOUPE MELON

3 TABLESPOONS OLIVE OIL

1 TABLESPOON MINCED FRESH

DILL

JUICE OF 1 LEMON

Wash and thinly slice the zucchini. Scoop into balls or cube the melon. In a frying pan heat the oil until just before it smokes, or to the smoking point. Add the zucchini, and season with salt and pepper. Add the minced dill and lemon juice. Cook until the zucchini turns a vivid green, then toss in the melon. Serve immediately.

DESSERTS

The apple was probably the single fruit that kept the Shakers' survival intact. They planted apple trees, cultivated them, grew apples, dried them, sold them, baked them, pressed them, boiled, froze, and candied them. For all of their different apple recipes, the one that is the most Shaker, to me, is the Rosewater Apple Pie. Eldress Bertha makes one that is perfect in taste, pie crust, tartness, sugar, and consistency every single time she does it. As far as I'm concerned, that's real talent.

BAKED APPLE CUSTARD TART
WITH ROSEWATER MERINGUE

SERVES 8

PASTRY CRUST

4 STICKS UNSALTED BUTTER	7 TABLESPOONS VERY COLD
4³/₄ CUPS FLOUR	BUTTERMILK
1 EGG YOLK	

In a mixing bowl blend the butter and flour to a mealy
consistency. Slowly add the egg yolk and buttermilk, mixing only
until the mixture comes together to form a ball. Roll the dough
out to a thickness of one-quarter inch. Line a pie tin with the
dough.

CUSTARD

4 EGGS	1 STICK UNSALTED BUTTER,
2 EGG YOLKS	MELTED
1 CUP GRANULATED SUGAR	CINNAMON TO TASTE

Combine all custard ingredients in a blender, and mix for
30 seconds. Set aside.

ROSEWATER MERINGUE

3 EGG WHITES

¼ CUP CONFECTIONERS' SUGAR

1 TEASPOON ROSE WATER

Slowly whip the egg whites, gradually adding the sugar. Add the rose water. Whip to stiff peaks.

TART PREPARATION

2 MEDIUM APPLES

PASTRY CRUST

CUSTARD

ROSEWATER MERINGUE

Wash, core, and slice the apples. Shingle the apple slices in the dough-lined pie tin. Pour the custard over the sliced apples. Bake in a 425° F oven for 10 minutes. Reduce the oven temperature to 300° F, and continue to bake 20 minutes or until custard is set. When custard is done, top with meringue, and return custard to 450° F oven to brown the meringue. Chill, slice, and serve.

We found a very small number of recipes for chocolate. It would appear that the kitchen favored natural fruit and squash flavors and fillings. We like them too, but we prefer chocolate. Sister Ethel keeps little stores of it around her kitchen and in her freezer, and would send over a tiny saucer, as though we were kittens, with six cold chocolates for the "kitchen." Eldress Bertha can't eat it anymore.

We had a wonderful summer with chocolate. The use of lavender in chocolate, if it's done correctly, can amaze you with a flavor you would never expect.

CHOCOLATE LAVENDER

FROZEN CUSTARD

SERVES 8

4 ONE-OUNCE SQUARES	1/4 CUP BROWN SUGAR
(1/4 POUND) BAKER'S	1 CUP HEAVY CREAM
CHOCOLATE	3 1/2 CUPS LIGHT CREAM
6 EGG YOLKS	2 CUPS MILK
1–1 1/2 CUPS GRANULATED	1/4 CUP CORNSTARCH
SUGAR	2–3 LAVENDER SPRIGS

Combine all of the ingredients in a saucepan. Slowly simmer until the mixture thickens, stirring often. Strain the mixture, and pour into a freezer container. Freeze until set. Scoop, and serve.

CHOCOLATE CHEESE TART
WITH RASPBERRY MOUSSE

SERVES 12

CHOCOLATE CHEESE FILLING

1/4 CUP FLOUR

8 EGGS

1 1/2 POUNDS CREAM CHEESE

2 CUPS GRANULATED SUGAR

8 ONE-OUNCE SQUARES BAKER'S
CHOCOLATE, MELTED

1 TABLESPOON VANILLA

Combine all of the ingredients in a food processor, and mix until smooth. Set aside.

RASPBERRY MOUSSE

1 PINT RASPBERRIES

1 CUP GRANULATED SUGAR

1 CUP WHITE WINE

2 PACKETS GELATIN

3 CUPS HEAVY CREAM

Simmer the raspberries in the sugar and wine until reduced by half. Stir in the gelatin, and chill for 15 minutes. Whip the cream, and fold into the chilled fruit mixture.

TART PREPARATION

CHOCOLATE CHEESE FILLING

PASTRY CRUST

RASPBERRY MOUSSE

1 PINT FRESH RASPBERRIES

Pour the Chocolate Cheese Filling into a 12-inch tart pan lined with a pastry crust. Bake in a 325° F oven for 40–50 minutes or until set. Chill. Using a pastry bag, pipe out rosettes of Raspberry Mousse to mark each slice of the tart, and top with fresh raspberries. Serve.

COCOA CHEESE TART

SERVES 12

2 TABLESPOONS VANILLA

6 EGGS

1/2 POUND CREAM CHEESE

2 CUPS HEAVY CREAM

1 CUP COCOA POWDER

1 1/2–2 CUPS GRANULATED

SUGAR

PASTRY CRUST

WHIPPED CREAM (OPTIONAL)

Combine the vanilla, eggs, cream cheese, heavy cream, cocoa powder, and sugar in a food processor, and mix until smooth. Pour the batter into a 12-inch tart shell lined with pastry crust. Bake in a 325° F oven for 40–50 minutes or until set. Chill. Serve plain or with a dollop of whipped cream.

CHOCOLATE HEAVEN TART

SERVES 12

½ CUP GRATED BITTERSWEET CHOCOLATE	8 EGGS
	1 POUND CREAM CHEESE
2 CUPS PECANS	1 CUP BROWN SUGAR
2 TABLESPOONS CINNAMON	1 TABLESPOON VANILLA
PASTRY CRUST	WHIPPED CREAM

CHOCOLATE GANACHE

¾ CUP HEAVY CREAM	1 POUND CHOCOLATE CHIPS

In a saucepan bring the heavy cream to a boil. Pour the hot cream over the chocolate chips, and stir until the chocolate is melted. Cool the ganache to room temperature.

Combine the bittersweet chocolate, pecans, and cinnamon in a food processor. Mix until finely ground. Spread the chocolate and pecan mixture over the bottom of a 12-inch tart pan lined with pastry crust. Combine the eggs, cream cheese, sugar, and vanilla in a food processor, and mix until smooth. Pour the batter over the chocolate in the tart shell. Bake in a 325° F oven for 40–50 minutes or until set. Chill the tart. Glaze the tart with the Chocolate Ganache, and chill. Slice, and serve with a dollop of whipped cream.

MOCHA HEAVEN PUDDING

SERVES 6–8

4 ONE-OUNCE SQUARES BAKER'S CHOCOLATE	2 CUPS HEAVY CREAM
	3/4 CUP CONFECTIONERS' SUGAR
8 EGG YOLKS	1 TABLESPOON CINNAMON
2 CUPS BROWN SUGAR	1 CUP FRESH RASPBERRIES
2 CUPS COFFEE	1 TEASPOON AMARETTO
3 TABLESPOONS CORNSTARCH	LIQUEUR PER SERVING

Combine the chocolate, egg yolks, brown sugar, coffee, and cornstarch in a double boiler. Cook the mixture until it thickens. Chill. Whip the heavy cream, confectioners' sugar, and cinnamon until medium-stiff peaks form. Gently fold and swirl the whipped cream into the chilled chocolate base to give it a marble effect. Pour the pudding into individual dishes, and refrigerate. To serve, garnish each pudding with a couple of fresh raspberries and the Amaretto liqueur.

SHAKER FRUIT TART

SERVES 12

CUSTARD

12-INCH PREBAKED TART SHELL

3 KIWIS, PEELED AND SLICED

1 PINT STRAWBERRIES, HULLED

AND SLICED

1 PINT BLUEBERRIES, PICKED

OVER AND WASHED

CUSTARD

2 LEMONS, SLICED AND SEEDED

$1/3$ CUP WHITE WINE

2 CUPS GRANULATED SUGAR

4 EGG YOLKS

1 PACKET GELATIN

1 QUART HEAVY CREAM

In a sauce pot simmer the lemons in the wine and sugar until reduced by half. In a food processor puree the lemon mixture while adding the egg yolks one at a time, then add the gelatin. Chill. Whip the heavy cream until medium-stiff peaks form. Gently fold the whipped cream into the lemon base.

TART PREPARATION

Pour custard into a 12-inch prebaked tart shell. Garnish with fresh fruit. Chill. Slice and serve.

APPLE CIDER CHEESE TART

SERVES 12

1 CUP APPLE JUICE	2 APPLES, FINELY CHOPPED
CONCENTRATE	4 EGGS
1¹/₂ POUNDS CREAM CHEESE	PASTRY CRUST

Combine the juice, cream cheese, apples, and eggs in a food processor, and blend until smooth. Pour the batter into a 12-inch tart pan lined with pastry crust. Bake in a 325° F oven for 40–50 minutes or until set. Chill. Slice and serve.

MAPLE SWEET-POTATO

CHEESE TART

SERVES 12

1 MEDIUM SWEET POTATO	1/4 CUP MOLASSES
4 EGGS	3/4 CUP MAPLE SYRUP
2 EGG YOLKS	1 CUP LIGHT CREAM OR
1 CUP CREAM CHEESE	BUTTERMILK
1 TABLESPOON CINNAMON	PASTRY CRUST
JUICE OF 1 LEMON	1 CUP BROWN SUGAR

Bake and peel the sweet potato. Combine all of the ingredients except the pastry crust and brown sugar in a food processor, and blend until smooth. Pour the batter into a 12-inch tart pan lined with the pastry crust. Bake in a 325° F oven for 40–50 minutes or until set. Halfway through baking sprinkle the tart with the brown sugar. Chill. Slice and serve.

LEMON LAVENDER TART

SERVES 12

8 EGGS	1 CUP CREAM CHEESE
1½ CUPS GRANULATED SUGAR	2 TABLESPOONS MINCED FRESH
1 LEMON, SEEDED AND SLICED	LAVENDER
½ CUP FRESH LEMON JUICE	PASTRY CRUST

Combine all of the ingredients except the pastry crust in a food processor, and blend until smooth. Pour the batter into a 12-inch tart pan lined with pastry crust. Bake in a 325° F oven for 40–45 minutes or until set. Chill. Serve each slice with Raspberry Puree or Red Wine Blueberry Clove Sauce.

RASPBERRY PURÉE

2 PINTS FRESH RASPBERRIES

WITH SUGAR TO TASTE

Puree in a blender until smooth.

RED WINE BLUEBERRY
CLOVE SAUCE

5 CUPS FRESH BLUEBERRIES,	1 CUP RED WINE
PICKED OVER AND	½ CUP GRANULATED SUGAR
WASHED	1 TEASPOON GROUND CLOVES

In a sauce pot simmer 3 cups of blueberries with the wine, sugar, and cloves until reduced by half. Puree the mixture in a blender until smooth. Chill. Stir in the remaining 2 cups of blueberries. Ready to serve.

SPANISH CREAM TART

SERVES 12

1 EIGHT-OUNCE BLOCK CREAM CHEESE	6 EGG WHITES
1½ CUPS GRANULATED SUGAR	CREAM OF TARTAR
6 EGG YOLKS	PASTRY CRUST
2 TABLESPOONS VANILLA	SLICED FRESH STRAWBERRIES
1 CUP HEAVY CREAM	WHIPPED CREAM

Cut the cream cheese into half-inch cubes and place in a food processor or electric mixer bowl. Add the sugar, and cream the mixture until smooth. Scrape down the sides of the mixing bowl with a rubber spatula. Add the egg yolks and vanilla, mixing until incorporated. Transfer this mixture to a larger bowl, stir in heavy cream. In a separate bowl whip the egg whites with a pinch of cream of tartar until medium-stiff peaks form. Gently fold a third of the whipped egg whites into the above base, then gently fold in the remaining whipped egg whites. Pour the batter into a 12-inch tart pan lined with pastry crust. Bake the tart in a 400° F oven for 10 minutes. Reduce the oven temperature to 275° F, and continue to bake 20–30 minutes or until custard is set. Chill 4 hours. Slice tart thinly, and serve with sliced fresh strawberries and whipped cream.

HONEY PEACH CREAM TART

SERVES 12

1 CUP HONEY

4 FRESH PEACHES, PITTED AND

    QUARTERED

4 EGGS

1/2 POUND CREAM CHEESE

JUICE OF 1 LEMON

PASTRY CRUST

Combine all of the ingredients except the pastry crust in a food processor, and blend until smooth. Pour the batter into a 12-inch tart pan lined with pastry crust. Bake in a 325° F oven for 40–50 minutes or until set. Chill. Slice and serve.

INDIAN PUDDING TART

WITH MAPLE APPLE ICE CREAM

———

SERVES 12

2 CUPS LIGHT CREAM	1 CUP SUGAR, BROWN OR
2 CUPS HEAVY CREAM	WHITE
5 TABLESPOONS CORNMEAL	2 APPLES, CORED AND SLICED
6 EGGS	PASTRY CRUST
3/4 CUP MOLASSES	

In a sauce pot scald the creams, and add the cornmeal. Cook for 5 minutes, stirring constantly. Combine the eggs, molasses, and sugar in a food processor, and blend until the mixture turns pale yellow. With the processor on, slowly add the warm cornmeal and cream mixture to finish the pudding. Place the sliced apples in a 12-inch tart pan lined with pastry crust. Pour the pudding over the sliced apples. Bake in a 325° F oven for 40–50 minutes or until set. Chill. Slice, and serve with Maple Apple Ice Cream, p. 184.

SOUFFLÉ ROULADE WITH

INDIAN PUDDING MOUSSE

SERVES 8–12

This may sound a little worldly for a Shaker kitchen, but we felt the Indian pudding vindicated us, since it is such an American food.

SOUFFLÉ

1¹/₂ CUPS MILK	5 TABLESPOONS FLOUR
3 TABLESPOONS GRANULATED SUGAR	5 EGG YOLKS
	1 TEASPOON VANILLA
¹/₂ STICK UNSALTED BUTTER	5 EGG WHITES

Scald the milk and sugar. Set aside. Melt the butter in a saucepan. Stir in the flour to form a paste. Slowly stir in the scalded milk and sugar, stirring until smooth. Cook until the mixture thickens, stirring often. Remove pan from the stove, and stir in the egg yolks one at a time. Stir in the vanilla. In a separate bowl, whip the egg whites to form medium-stiff peaks. Gently fold the whipped egg whites into the soufflé base. Pour into a parchment-lined and buttered half sheet pan (12" x 17"). Bake in a 400° F oven 15–20 minutes until lightly browned. Remove from the oven, and chill.

INDIAN PUDDING MOUSSE

1 CUP LIGHT CREAM	6 EGG YOLKS
1 CUP GRANULATED SUGAR	1 PACKET GELATIN
1/4 CUP MOLASSES	1 QUART HEAVY CREAM
1/4 CUP CORNMEAL	

In a sauce pot scald the cream, sugar, and molasses. Add the cornmeal, and cook 5 minutes, stirring constantly. Remove pot from stove, and stir in the egg yolks one at a time. Stir in the gelatin, and cool the mixture. Whip the heavy cream until medium-stiff peaks form. Gently fold the whipped cream into the cool pudding base.

SOUFFLÉ PREPARATION

Remove the chilled soufflé from the sheet pan, and gently peel back the parchment paper. Set the soufflé sheet on top of the parchment paper (the paper will make it a little easier to roll the soufflé). Spread the Indian Pudding Mousse evenly over the soufflé sheet. Starting at one end, gently roll up the mousse in the soufflé (just like rolling a jelly roll cake). Chill. Slice and serve with kiwi puree and strawberries or with a lemon curd sauce.

PUMPKIN TART

SERVES 12

1 CUP PUMPKIN PUREE

3/4–1 CUP GRANULATED SUGAR

4 EGGS

2 CUPS BUTTERMILK

1/2 CUP MOLASSES

JUICE OF 1 LEMON

2 TEASPOONS CINNAMON

PASTRY CRUST

WHIPPED CREAM

Combine all of the ingredients except the pastry crust and whipped cream in a food processor, and blend until smooth. Pour the custard into a 12-inch tart pan lined with pastry crust. Bake in a 325° F oven for 40–50 minutes or until set. Chill. Slice, and serve with a dollop of whipped cream.

FALLEN SOUFFLÉ ROLLED WITH

A SWEET-POTATO MOUSSE

SERVES 8–12

SWEET-POTATO MOUSSE

2 PACKETS GELATIN

$^1/_2$ CUP COLD WATER

2 CUPS SWEET-POTATO PUREE

$^1/_2$–$^3/_4$ CUP BROWN SUGAR

1$^1/_2$ TEASPOONS VANILLA

1$^1/_2$ TEASPOONS CINNAMON

3 CUPS HEAVY CREAM

Soak the gelatin in the cold water. In a food processor, combine the sweet-potato puree, brown sugar, vanilla, and cinnamon, blending until smooth. Heat the gelatin to 110° F, when it just starts to melt. In a mixer, combine the sweet-potato mixture with the heavy cream. Start to whip, then slowly add the melted gelatin. Whip until medium-stiff peaks form. Follow the directions for Soufflé Preparation, p. 181. Serve with whipped cream instead of fruit.

ICE CREAMS AND SHERBETS

———

The Shakers also made sherbets and ice creams. When a Shaker recipe calls for heavy cream, it means a whole different thing than that little carton of "ultraprocessed" you get at the corner store. So, in these recipes use the best cream you can find, and I promise you these will be great desserts.

Jeffrey is really the ice cream creator. I came up with a few concoctions, but Jeffrey knows how to put it all together. It was, in fact, his Twenty-five Percent Butterfat Chocolate Ice Cream that first made me regard him as a serious cook. Jeffrey has a remarkable sense of taste and texture combinations and is completely fearless in the kitchen. Some of the following recipes are the proof.

MAPLE APPLE ICE CREAM

———

YIELDS 2¹/₂ QUARTS

1 QUART HEAVY CREAM	12 EGG YOLKS
1 QUART LIGHT CREAM	1 TABLESPOON VANILLA
2 CUPS MAPLE SUGAR	4 GRATED SWEET APPLES

In a sauce pot scald the creams with 1 cup of the maple sugar. In a mixing bowl whip the egg yolks with the remaining 1 cup maple sugar until the mixture turns pale yellow. Slowly add the scalded cream as you continue to whip the sugar and egg mixture. Transfer the mixture to a double boiler, and cook until it thickens (coats the back of a spoon), stirring often. Add the vanilla, and refrigerate overnight. Fold the grated apples into the cold ice cream base. Freeze according to manufacturer's directions for your ice cream freezer. Serve with Indian Pudding Tart, p. 179.

BANANA CHOCOLATE

ICE CREAM WITH PECANS

YIELDS 1 1/2 QUARTS

4 1/2 CUPS HEAVY CREAM	1/4 CUP BANANA LIQUEUR
3 CUPS GRANULATED SUGAR	1 TABLESPOON VANILLA
9 EGG YOLKS	1 CUP CHOCOLATE CHIPS
6 MEDIUM BANANAS	1/2 CUP PECAN PIECES

Scald the cream with 1 1/2 cups of the sugar. In a separate bowl whip the egg yolks with the remaining 1 1/2 cups sugar until the mixture turns pale yellow. Slowly add the scalded cream as you continue to whip the sugar and egg mixture. Transfer this mixture to a double boiler, and cook until it thickens (coats the back of a spoon), stirring often. Peel the bananas and puree them with the banana liqueur and vanilla. Remove cream mixture from the double boiler, put in a bowl, stir in the banana puree, and refrigerate overnight. Freeze according to manufacturer's directions for your ice cream freezer. Halfway through the freezing process add the chocolate chips and pecan pieces, then continue the freezing process. Harden the ice cream 24 hours before serving.

WILD MAINE BLUEBERRY

LAVENDER ICE CREAM

---

1 PINT WILD BLUEBERRIES, PICKED OVER AND WASHED

1/4 CUP MAPLE SYRUP

1 QUART HEAVY CREAM

2 CUPS GRANULATED SUGAR

4 FRESH LAVENDER SPRIGS

9 EGG YOLKS

Simmer the blueberries in the maple syrup until they burst, then puree. Scald the cream with half of the sugar and the lavender sprigs. In a separate bowl whip the egg yolks with the remaining 1 cup sugar until the mixture turns pale yellow. Strain the scalded cream, and slowly add it as you continue to whip the sugar and egg mixture. Transfer the mixture to a double boiler and cook until it thickens (coats the back of a spoon), stirring often. Remove from the double boiler, put in a bowl and stir in the blueberry puree, and refrigerate overnight. Freeze according to manufacturer's directions for your ice cream freezer. Harden 24 hours before serving.

BLUEBERRY MAPLE

ICE CREAM

YIELDS 1 1/2 QUARTS

2 CUPS FRESH BLUEBERRIES,
    PICKED OVER AND WASHED

1 CUP MAPLE SUGAR

2 CUPS HEAVY CREAM

2 CUPS LIGHT CREAM

6 EGG YOLKS

1 TEASPOON VANILLA

Follow the procedure for the Wild Maine Blueberry Lavender Ice Cream, p. 186.

CHOCOLATE LAVENDER

ICE CREAM

YIELDS 1¹/₂ QUARTS

2 CUPS HEAVY CREAM

2 CUPS LIGHT CREAM

1¹/₄ CUPS GRANULATED SUGAR

3–5 FRESH LAVENDER SPRIGS

8 EGG YOLKS

1 TABLESPOON VANILLA

1 STICK UNSALTED BUTTER,

   IN SMALL PIECES

1 POUND BITTERSWEET

   CHOCOLATE, IN VERY

   SMALL PIECES

Scald the creams with half of the sugar and the lavender. Strain the scalded cream. In a separate bowl whip the egg yolks with the remaining sugar until the mixture turns pale yellow. Slowly add the scalded cream as you continue to whip the sugar and egg mixture. Transfer the mixture to a double boiler, and cook until the mixture thickens (coats the back of a spoon), stirring often. Remove pan from the stove, and stir in the vanilla and the butter one piece at a time until incorporated. Stir constantly. Put the chocolate pieces in a bowl. Pour the warm cream base over the chocolate, and stir until the chocolate melts. Refrigerate overnight. Freeze according to manufacturer's directions for your ice cream freezer. Harden 24 hours before serving.

DRAMBUIE PLUM ICE CREAM

YIELDS 1 1/2 QUARTS

12 PLUMS, PITTED	2 1/2 CUPS HEAVY CREAM
1/2 CUP WATER	1 1/2 CUPS GRANULATED SUGAR
2 TABLESPOONS HONEY	5 EGG YOLKS
1/4 CUP DRAMBUIE	1 TEASPOON VANILLA

In a saucepan cook the plums in water, honey, and Drambuie until soft. Puree the plums. Scald the cream with 3/4 cup of the sugar. In a separate bowl whip the egg yolks with the remaining 3/4 cup sugar until the mixture turns pale yellow. Slowly add the scalded cream to the eggs as you continue to whip. Transfer this mixture to a double boiler, and cook until it thickens (coats the back of a spoon), stirring often. Remove pan from the stove, and stir in the plum puree and vanilla. Freeze according to manufacturer's directions for your ice cream freezer. Harden 24 hours before serving.

REAL MAPLE WALNUT

ICE CREAM

YIELDS 1 QUART

2 CUPS HEAVY CREAM	6 EGG YOLKS
2 CUPS LIGHT CREAM	1 TEASPOON VANILLA
1 CUP MAPLE SUGAR	1 CUP WALNUT PIECES

Follow the procedure for Banana Chocolate Ice Cream with Pecans, p. 185.

HONEY SPICE VANILLA

ICE CREAM

2 CUPS HEAVY CREAM	1 TABLESPOON CINNAMON
2 CUPS LIGHT CREAM	2 TEASPOONS GROUND GINGER
3/4 CUP GRANULATED SUGAR	2 TEASPOONS NUTMEG
9 EGG YOLKS	1/2 STICK UNSALTED BUTTER,
1/2 CUP HONEY	IN SMALL PIECES
2 TABLESPOONS VANILLA	

Scald the creams with half of the sugar. In a separate bowl whip the egg yolks with the remaining sugar until the mixture turns pale yellow. Slowly add the scalded cream as you continue to whip the sugar and egg mixture. Transfer the mixture to a double boiler, and cook until it thickens (coats the back of a spoon), stirring often. Remove from the stove, and stir in the honey, vanilla, spices, and butter one piece at a time until incorporated. Stir constantly. Refrigerate overnight. Freeze according to manufacturer's directions for your ice cream freezer. Harden 24 hours before serving.

ORANGE RHUBARB SHERBET

3 CUPS DICED RHUBARB

1 ORANGE, SLICED AND SEEDED

2 CUPS GRANULATED SUGAR

3 TABLESPOONS ORANGE JUICE
CONCENTRATE

1 QUART WATER

6 EGG WHITES

Combine the rhubarb, orange slices, sugar, orange juice concentrate, and water in a saucepan. Simmer until the rhubarb becomes very soft. Puree the mixture in a blender until smooth. Refrigerate overnight. In a separate bowl whip the egg whites to form medium-stiff peaks. Gently fold the whipped egg whites into the cold sherbet base. Freeze according to manufacturer's directions for your ice cream freezer. Remove sherbet from freezer 30 minutes before serving, and allow to soften in refrigerator. Serve.

STRAWBERRY RHUBARB

SHERBET

_____

YIELDS 1 1/2 QUARTS

3 CUPS DICED RHUBARB	1 1/2 CUPS GRANULATED SUGAR
2 CUPS SLICED FRESH	1 QUART WATER
STRAWBERRIES	6 EGG WHITES

Follow the procedure for Orange Rhubarb Sherbet, p. 192, adding the strawberries with the rhubarb, and omitting the orange slices and orange juice concentrate.

BUTTERS

The Shakers used creams, heavy, soured, and whipped, in so many dishes, ate cheese and drank lots of milk, and made their own butter, which they generously used. One can only wonder with all the reports on cholesterol and fats why the Shakers enjoyed such good health and longevity.

While cooking at the Creamery we also made our own butter. Not in a churn, but in a food processor. The "process," no pun intended, is very simple. Put 2 pints of heavy cream into your food processor with the processing blade, turn it on, and let it go until it whips the cream into a butter ball. Remove it from the machine, and squeeze as much milk from the butter as you can. Break it into small pieces, and return it to the processor. Still using the chopping blade, add the flavorings. This time add 1/4 cup fresh blueberries, 2 tablespoons honey, 1 teaspoon of ground cloves. Process until the butter is creamy and the herbs are well integrated. Refrigerate.

Since the process is so basic, I don't feel I need to write it out for each group of flavorings. What I would like to do is give you a list of combinations. The measurements will always be the same. Or, of course, try whatever you like!

LAVENDER FIG

HONEY LAVENDER PEAR

MAPLE PECAN

SPEARMINT HONEY

TOMATO BASIL

GINGER HONEY WALNUT

POPPY SEED ORANGE

CHIVE WITH MARJORAM
FLOWER GARNISH

GINGER HONEY PEACH

BASIL SAGE

BLUEBERRY MAPLE

KIWI LAVENDER

NASTURTIUM HONEY
SPEARMINT

HONEY PLUM

MAPLE ORANGE

NASTURTIUM CHIVE

BLUEBERRY LAVENDER

EPILOGUE

It has surely been a great privilege to know the Shaker Sisters, to have spent time in their surroundings, to have seen the pieces of their world that are still intact, and to have stood and worked and walked on the same floors as so many generations of Shakers have. I don't know what kind of effect this is supposed to have on a person, but I feel somehow calmed by the experience. Maybe it was being in such close proximity to the remnants of the Shakers' perfect order. Maybe it is two ladies who hold my hand into a past that ends with them. One day my perception will blur and fade and they will disappear a little more—that to me is the real secret of life.

When I first wandered up Shaker Road and met Bertha, I remember the conversation as I was leaving. I said to her, "The Shakers are so wonderful, they've accomplished so much, and their way of life seems so ideal. Why is it being allowed to come to a conclusion?" Bertha smiled with patience and answered, "Every thing, like every body, has its own time. It is born, grows and makes its statement, and passes. If you want to be a Shaker, be a Shaker in your own house."

I think a good place to begin is in the kitchen.

KITCHEN CLOSED.

INDEX

Custard, sweet
  frozen, chocolate lavender, 168
  in pie, apple, 166
  in pie, fruit, 173

D

DAIRY PRODUCTS, about, x, xi, xxi, 18, 94;
    substitutions for, xxi.
    See also individual names.
DESSERTS, 165–193. *See also* individual names.
Drambuie Plum Ice Cream, 189
DRESSING. *See* Salad Dressing; Sauce; Stuffing.
Duck
    breast, grilled, 80
    pâté, and pear, 82
Duckling
    roast, in glaze, blueberry lemonade, 78
    roast, in glaze, ginger cider, 76
    roast, in glaze, honey crab apple, 79
    roast, in glaze, raspberry maple, 77
    to roast, 75

E

ENTRÉES, 47–127

F

Fennel, in butter, red pepper, 135
FISH, 49–74. *See also* individual names and
    Shellfish.
    casserole, seafood, in sauce, ginger cider,
      72
    catfish, pan-fried in mayonnaise, in sauce,
      lemon custard, 59
    chowder, salmon, sherried, chilled, 20
    chowder, Shaker-style, 13
    cod, baked, with mousse, salmon, in cider
      butter, 71
    moussse, salmon, 71
    salmon, baked, in sauce, bacon potato, 54
    salmon, baked, with pâté, lobster, in herb
      sauce, 50
    salmon, baked, with peas and onions, in
      cream sauce, 52
    salmon, in soup, sorrel, chilled, 16
    salmon, sauce, 70
    salmon, steaks, pan-fried in butter, lime
      basil, 53
    salmon, stuffing, 66
    sole, baked, in sauce, Frangelico peach
      hazelnut, 64
    sole, baked, in sauce, lobster nasturtium,
      65
    sole, baked, in sauce, salmon buttermilk,
      70
    sole, baked, with stuffing, salmon, in sauce,
      cider Hollandaise, 66
    sole, baked, with stuffing, shrimp pâté, in
      lobster sauce, 68

swordfish, in sauce, curry, with almonds
      and coconut, 74
    turbot, baked, in sauce, sorrel cream, 61
Frangelico Peach sauce, 64
FRUIT. *See also* individual names.
    pie, custard, 173
    salad, with mayonnaise, lavender honey, 45

G

Ganache, chocolate, 171
Ginger
    dressing, sweet-sour, 28
    in glaze, cider, 76
    sauce, 134
    sauce, apple butter, 57, 137
    in sauce, cider sour cream, 72
GLAZE. *See* Sauce.
Graham, Sylvester, xi
GRAVY. *See* Sauce. *Also see* glazes.
Greene, Sister Edith, 47

H

Ham
    baked, in glaze, blackberry raspberry red
      wine, 127
    baked, in glaze, cider, 126
HERB, about, xx, xxi. *See also* individual
    names.
    broth, 9
    dressing, maple syrup, 23
    oil, olive, 133
    sauce, cream, for fish, 50
    sauce, sour cream, 146
    sauce, white wine, for pot roast, 106
Hollandaise sauce, cider, 67
Honey
    dressing, lime 42
    glaze, crab apple, 79
    mayonnaise, with lavender, 45
Honey Peach Cream Tart, 178
Honey Spice Vanilla Ice Cream, 191
Horseradish, in sauce, raspberry, 113
Hudson, Sister Ethel, xiv, xv, xvii, xviii

I

ICE CREAM. *See also* Custard, frozen; Sherbet;
    Sorbet.
    banana chocolate pecan, 185
    blueberry maple, 187
    blueberry, wild, with lavender, 186
    chocolate lavender, 188
    Drambuie plum, 189
    honey spice vanilla, 191
    maple apple, 184
    maple walnut, 190
Indian pudding
    mousse, 181
    pie, 171